Hidden Treasures in Dark Places

By
VELMA HAGAR

Disclaimer: References to Scripture are the author's paraphrase.

Cover Photo: Stacey Mills

Hardcover: ISBN: 978-0-9981828-2-7
Paperback: ISBN: 978-0-9981828-3-4
eBook ISBN: 978-0-9981828-4-1

Published in the United States of America
Printed in the United States of America.

Dedication

I DEDICATE THIS book to my ten grandchildren. In the beginning when I first began writing my blog, I was writing to them. I wanted them to get a scripture every single day, and I wanted to give it to them in a life-application form. So I kept it simple, and I texted them this little short blog every day.

Eventually I put all the blogs into a book form, and *Hidden Treasures in Secret Places* was born. Since then, I have continued to write that blog every single day without fail for the last 15 years. These children have grown into adults and are not only my grandchildren but they are my confidantes, many times my recreation, and most of all my amazing friends.

This sequel to *Hidden Treasures in Secret Places* is still formatted in a daily devotional style of short blogs that include a life-application example, as well as a daily scripture. It is "unchurchy" yet profound. It is filled with the treasures that can be found in every dark situation. I still contend that there are treasures everywhere, and the only criteria to finding them is you must look for them.

"I will give you hidden treasures, stored in dark secret places, so that you may know that I am the Lord."

Poems for my ten grandchildren

My grandsons

When it comes to grandsons, I only have three, each one is different but so special to me.

The oldest one Tom sings like a bird, he's handsome and dapper and is good with words, he definitely has the Midas touch, and I certainly love him ever so much.

Next came Josiah who does everything right, he's a wonderful husband and father and serves God with all his might.

Last but not least is my own little Jack, who you can often find at the caddy shack...he gets holes in one and hits the ball like a pro, straight to the top this boy will go.

I love to share a cuppa java with each of my guys, they are all three handsome, witty, and wise...

My three little gems...are a sparkling light that adds joy to my days and peace to my nights.

All is well with my soul.

My granddaughters

Seven granddaughters have I and oh what a blast,
Like a movie set with each character cast.
There's Erica at the start who has a strong mind,
She's clever and crafty, feisty yet kind.
Next came Hannah girl, unique and that's for sure,
She sings like a bird and has a heart that's sweet
and pure.
Then came our Jilliann with Uncle Sam's hair,
Beautiful and sensitive, she and Hannah are a pair.
Then came Nicole who loves to run the show,
At problem solving, she's truly a pro.
Emily entered as a dancer from the start,
Blond and beautiful and can melt your heart.
Then came Gracie, who is smart as a whip,
Dazzling us all with her amazing quips.
Last but not least, Audrey completed the run,
With the heart of a servant, yet lively and fun.
It moves me to tears when I think of my girls...
A beautiful strand of perfectly matched pearls.

This book is based on Scripture, Isaiah 45:3

*"I will give you the treasures of darkness and
hidden riches of secret places."*

Foreword

by Sammy Hagar, aka the Red Rocker

THERE WERE FOUR of us in the Hagar clan. The oldest was our sister Bobbi, second was Velma, brother Bob, or Junior, was third, and last but not least, myself. You would have thought the pecking order would be pretty much in that order, and even though our sister Bobbi was the bossy one, Velma always seemed to end up getting what she wanted first, and even when it came to family chores, she seemed to do less and get paid the same as everyone else and sometimes even more. She had a special way with money, even as a child. Mom always said, "She could make a nickel seem like a dime." Why, you ask, did she get by with everything? Because she was smarter than the rest of us! She was always the drama queen, saying things like "I'm not feeling good today. Would someone bring me a glass of water?" She slept in late and then would complain because the family made too much noise in the morning. She pretty much ran the show at home. Even though Bobbi was the bossy one, Velma always found a way to get her own way. She invented her own language once, and she would spell the words backwards and say them backwards faster than the rest of us could do it forward... She always had a brilliant mind and a wonderful imagination.

One of my favorite things that she wrote that I still repeat today is a poem she wrote in her early teens that said absolutely nothing. Every word was a contradiction. I once stole one of her essays that she had written in middle school and used it for a project in the 7th grade, and I got an A+ The only one I ever got in school. Most of you would probably think I was the oddball in the family, but without a doubt, it was Velma. I'm not sure what took her so long to finally write a book, but now she's doing her second one, and I assure you it will entertain and encourage you as it draws you towards a richer life.

Good job, sis.

Sammy Hagar, aka the Red Rocker

Foreword

AS A FAN of both Velma Hagar and her first book, *Hidden Treasures in Secret Places*, I am reminded of the life-transforming power of daily devotionals. My decision to devote my first morning thoughts to God and his ways have divinely changed my life "one day at a time." My journey to a life of faith has taught me God doesn't enlarge my faith or my territory instantly; it's a slow, daily process that has happened over my lifetime. It could not have happened without the unshakeable godly wisdom of devotionals such as *Hidden Treasures in Secret Places* or Velma's newest daily devotional *Hidden Treasures in Dark Places*.

The false light of the world that drew me in brought me only to darkness. But it was the love of God, found even in the darkness, that broke my heart. Brokenness was a necessary part of my journey. God's love for me was revealed in the darkness of my own life and by the divine contrast between the lies of my old beliefs and the truth of God's Word.

Today, due to books such as Velma's and her steadfast faith, my purposes in life are simple: to simply be the best husband, father, and friend I can be and to shine the light of God in an ever-darkening world. For flawed men such as me, my life purpose need not be any more complicated than that. I thank you, Velma, for all your kindness, love, and the wisdom contained in your God-inspired books.

Blessings to you all

> Tony C.-Author: The Wise Man & the
> Fool: tonyc@wisemanfool.com

Introduction

*Isaiah 45:3 says, "I will give you hidden treasures,
riches stored in dark secret places, so that you may
know that I am the Lord."*

HIDDEN TREASURES IN Dark Places is a sequel
to my first book, *Hidden Treasures in Secret Places*.
After I wrote my first book, I never would've thought in
a million years that I would be writing a second book,
especially because I am in my late seventies. But I read
a poem called "The Bridge Builder" (you can read it at
the back of this book), and that poem speaks of an old
man who is crossing a dangerous chasm in the dark,
latter years of his life, and after he has made it safely to
the other side, he stops and builds a bridge for those
who are coming after him. He builds the bridge so that
those coming behind will have a safer passage. This
story moved me to tears, and I realized it doesn't matter
how old I am because the words of my book are meant
to guide and help others.

When I turned sixty, I began writing a blog to
my children and grandchildren every day, and that
blog eventually turned into my first book. I have had
wonderful success with *Hidden Treasures in Secret*

Places. It was based on the scripture that says, "I will show you hidden treasures in dark secret places," and since our times are troubled and somewhat dark, I felt we would focus on the "hidden treasures in dark places" this time.

I have safely journeyed through life, and my life has been filled with lots of troubled waters, and I have learned much. I have learned it doesn't matter where you start in life but rather where you finish. When those behind you remember you, they will remember the way you ended your life rather than the way you began. Your legacy will be a compilation of what you have come to in your end.

I started with a very troubled life. I had a psychotic, alcoholic father who instilled fear in me so deep that I spent many of my adult years working through those fears, and eventually "I called unto God, and he delivered me from all my fears." It was a journey as opposed to an event. As I continued to seek God, all my fears were eventually removed, one by one. Today I am a very brave woman with only the fear of not pleasing God. The desire of my heart is to pass on this beautiful legacy God has provided for me to my grand-children and all those who come after me. To learn from my words rather than have to deal with any of the horrors of life. Life is amazingly beautiful when we choose to apply God's word.

I was forty before I gave my life over to Jesus, and "my latter years have truly been better than my former years," just as God promises. There are over six thousand promises in the Bible, and if we learn to apply them and remind God of those promises, life becomes so beautiful. The colors are brighter, the flowers smell sweeter, and there is a joy and a peace and a sense of appreciation in your heart that goes beyond understanding. Both of my books are formatted in a daily devotional style, and every entry is based on a scripture. "The word never comes back void," so faithful reading of my book will produce godly wisdom. But I still want to encourage my readers to read the Bible because it is your book of instruction. Find your own hidden treasures in the promises strewn throughout God's word, as well as along your path of life. You have to look for the treasures to find them, but they are everywhere! They are even in the dark and mean things; they are even in the mud and scum of things. I have trained myself throughout my life to watch for treasures and to try to find those treasures in the dark and mean things and places. I promise you that if you will truly watch for "hidden treasures in dark secret places," you will find them. And when you find one, remember me, even when I'm dancing on the streets of gold in heaven. I pray your journey is safer because of this bridge I have built for you. "Here's looking at you, kid."

January

AS WE BEGIN our new year, we open with a clean slate, "forgetting things that are behind and looking towards the things that are ahead." We are not defined by our past, but rather, our past prepares us for our future. Begin the new year by putting your valuable training into good use by helping yourself and others. "The iron that has been through the fire is the strongest." Have a blessed year.

EMBRACE CHANGE AS we enter the new year. Change is inevitable, as we are in a continuous state of transition. Nothing in your physical, natural existence is immutable. Expect the new year to be the year of discovery. Remember you only get what you expect. Make a resolution this year to seek out and apply some of the six thousand promises in God's Word. Read them and put your name on them as you walk out the victorious life God has promised those who seek him. "Forget those things that are behind, and look towards those things that are ahead."

Day 2   January 2

THERE CAN BE a power in your darkest hour. I believe that more people turn to God in dark hours. Those times when a person feels hopeless and helpless can be your turning point. "In your weakness, God is made strong." When there is nowhere else to turn, people will turn to God, making these times a high point in your life. Stay encouraged. It is often the darkest just before the dawn.

THE LACK OF self-control is the evidence of allowing your carnal nature to rule. Remember self-control is a fruit of the spirit and God tells us to "walk in the spirit and we will not fulfill the lusts of the flesh." Control your flesh! If you let the arm of the flesh control your life, you will get into trouble every time. "The flesh is weak, but the spirit is strong." Submit your life to God and allow the spirit to rule. Take charge of your flesh before it takes charge of you! The flesh rarely makes good choices until you whip it into submission.

Day 3 January 3

THE THINGS WE see with our eyes are only part of the truth. There is a very real world that cannot be seen with our eyes. And to deny that the devil or spirit realm is real is about as logical as going into the slums at night while swinging your wallet over your head. The devil is very real, and he "prowls around seeking whom he may devour." Your ignorance of the evil spirit world makes you easy prey. Trust God and "resist the devil and he will flee from you."

LAUGHTER LOWERS BLOOD pressure, and it is contagious. "A merry heart does good like a medicine." If you do not have people around you who you laugh with, you need to find new companions. God gave us laughter as a joy and a medicine. People are so willing to take pills, when in truth, they just need a good belly laugh. God provided mankind with everything he needs for a happy healthy life. Walk in his plan for you. Laugh out loud often!

DAY 4   January 4

SMALL CORRECTIONS CAN make a huge difference. It is the small things in life that make up the whole of your life. Our tendency is to overcorrect, when in fact, a very small detail can change the whole outcome of something. When you look at a project of any kind, take the next small step towards it! When you picture the whole project, it becomes overwhelming, and many times you don't do anything. "If you are faithful with a little, you will become ruler over much."

WE HAVE ALL had our failures, but God is willing to totally forgive "and not even remember your sin anymore." How about you, can you forget and forgive yourself? Your failures will only make you stronger if you will accept the forgiveness that Jesus provided on the cross. "Forget those things that are behind and look towards those things that are ahead." And always remember it is not how you started that matters but rather how you finish.

Day 5   January 5

RESENTMENT CAN ONLY *destroy, just as love can only restore.* What a contrast this is. Love will always restore whatever has been broken in relationships, while resentment will eat away at relationships. Always clear the air and do not let resentment settle into your soul, or it will destroy you from the inside out. "Faith, hope, and love, but the greatest of these is love." Love conquers everything. Operate in it as you go through your life.

NEVER LET THE pain of your past block the blessings of your future. In fact, the pain from your past enables you to appreciate the good that comes along. Those who have never endured trials do not know how to appreciate what they have. God's Word says, "It is good for a man to carry the yoke in his youth." Don't sit around and whine about what you went through as a child. Instead, use it as a learning curve for the future.

DAY 6   January 6

DO NOT THINK intently on things that rob you of your faith. You do not need to deny the facts, but do not think intently on them. "Keep your eyes on the things above and not on the things below." "As a man thinks, so he is." Control your thinking! "Cast down wild imaginings and anything that exalts itself above the Word of God." Think on things that are lovely, noble, beautiful, sweet, and good.

MAN IS THE only one of God's creations that has the gift of speech, and in that gift lies "the power of life and death." Use your tongue wisely because, eventually, if you say things often enough, they will come to pass. God says that "he will create whatever you say with your mouth." You are literally a composite of everything you have ever spoken. Change your words, and you will change your life!

DAY 7   January 7

MAKE ALL EFFORT not to judge or condemn because God's Word says "when you judge you will be judged, and when you condemn, you will be condemned." Consider this before you decide to blast others. God's Word is true whether you believe it or not, and you can enhance all your days by following the parameters that God has set for our lives. Judging and condemning is out of those parameters. Play nice!

"IF I COULD just touch the hem of his garment, I will be healed." Notice how the woman with the issue of blood in the Bible had to confess out loud and then believe she would be healed before it happened. There were hundreds of people following Jesus that day, and all of them were touching him. But this woman confessed out loud that if she could touch him, she would be healed. Your words can change your life! Start confessing out loud the promises of God and then stand and believe them. "As you believe, it is done unto you"

Day 8   January 8

WE ARE NOT a bunch of victims! If you have claimed Jesus as your Savior, you have the power of life and death in that name! "Every knee will bow to the name of Jesus," including alcoholism, drug abuse, sexual immorality, sickness, poverty, absolutely everything! When was the last time you spoke to these things in your life or in the life of your children or grandchildren and told them to get out? "Whatever you say with your mouth, you shall have." "You shall eat the fruit of your lips."

GOD CREATES, FORMS, fashions, and molds the words of your lips. He literally creates that which you keep speaking. Holy Toledo, if that doesn't scare you, I don't know what should. What has been coming out of your mouth? "I create the fruit of your lips." Whatever you consistently confess, praise, or pray for, God will create in your life. Make positive confessions with your mouth and then "hold fast to your confessions."

THE LIES IN your life are clues to what God is doing. When the enemy attacks you in a certain area, stop and analyze what is happening and ask God what he is doing in that area for you. Remember the enemy only attacks where there is a treasure. Do not be overwhelmed because the enemy doesn't have any new tricks. He always attacks in the area where God is going to do something wonderful. Be encouraged. "Resist the devil, and he will flee from you.

DOUBT CAN THINK yourself right out of faith, and logic can destroy your faith! Faith is a choice. Choose to believe and do not allow logic, doubt, science, words, or anything else to rob you of your God-given faith. God gave all of us the same measure of faith, and it is up to us to develop and grow that faith, which has the potential to move a mountain. "Only believe."

DAY 10   January 10

FEAR WILL RENDER you crippled! We all have fears of some kind or another, but God tells us to "be strong and courageous." You have got to move forward with courage no matter what you are feeling. Courage is being proactive, even in the midst of great trials. Courage does not curl up in a ball and stay home. You have got to fight your own giants! Others can help with suggestions, but ultimately it is your battle, and with God's help, you will win. Courage will always defeat fear! "Call unto me, and I will deliver you from all of your fears."

WORDS MULTIPLY AND reproduce, and those seeds of words actually produce fruit, whether it be good fruit or bad fruit. Words are powerful! A proclamation made with the mouth will seal the words that were proclaimed. Be very careful what you say. "Your words have the power to set your life on a course of destruction," but they can also set your life on a course of success. "The power of life and death is in the tongue."

Day 11   January 11

THE GREATEST DANGER for winners is instability. Potential is lost when you are unstable or you waiver or take on the ways of bad company. The greatest danger to winners is hanging out and associating with the wrong people. Negative people will make you settle for less, and dream killers will destroy you. "Be not deceived, bad company corrupts good behavior." Get away from negative people if you want to be successful.

WHEN YOU TAKE ownership of something, it brings a settling of chaos. When you take control, you can form your life and become who you are meant to be. Set boundaries and subdue your own life. Learn by watching and tend your own garden. Water it, fertilize it, weed it, and it will produce a bountiful harvest. As much is within your control, take charge! "The wise man learns by watching while a fool has to have a rod taken to his back."

DAY 12   January 12

CHAOS, TOXICITY, ANGER, lawlessness, all comes from the enemy. He loves to distract with drama, and "he roams around seeking whom he may destroy." He is real, and he loves it when people do not think he is. "He is crouching at your doorstep," waiting for you to enter his realm by creating chaos and sin in your space. "Resist the devil, and he will flee from you."

RECOGNIZE THE SEASON you are in and live accordingly. "There is a time and a season for everything" If you try to live in a season that is not right yet, you will live in chaos. Operate in the correct season, and life will be more peaceful. Every season is beautiful if you accept the boundaries of that season. Enjoy the moment, savor each season of your life, and live your life appropriately.

DAY 13   January 13

OPERATE IN YOUR purpose and recognize your value and worth. God has you covered from birth to death. You are the height of his creation. Always keep that in mind. "His eye is on the sparrow," but it is much more on you. Walk out your life with the blessed assurance that God loves you no matter what.

GOD SPOKE THE universe into existence, and that is the magnificent power of words. Even though we do not have the power that God has, he tells us that "the power of life and death are in the tongue." He also says we can speak to the mountain and tell it to be removed, and if we believe, it must move. Imagine if we couple faith and our tongue: we could move mountains! Every problem in your life is a mountain. Speak to them and then believe.

Day 14   January 14

LIFE IS FILLED with storms, and they will never end until we get to heaven. But no matter what storm comes upon you, Jesus will walk through those storms with you, and he will work them towards good if you believe and are called according to His purpose for you. Jesus is an anchor that stabilizes you through every storm. "He promises to never leave you or forsake you." *All is well with my soul.*

GOD WILL OFTEN circle back to things in your life that were chaotic and confused, and he can fill them with life, joy, and peace as he fills your life with blessings. Live in the season that you are in, and "God will bring order to the chaos." We are called to a life of peace, and ofttimes God will circle back to unfinished business in our life, and you will be surprised at the outcome of something you thought was done. "There is a time and a season for everything under the sun."

Day 15   January 15

GOD HAS AN amazingly good plan for your life, but you can completely destroy that plan by holding unforgiveness! Just imagine what you are giving up when you hang on to that ugly, nonproductive, destructive, demonic unforgiveness! I have watched people grow old hanging on to their anger as it makes their life miserable, and yet they refuse to forgive. "God has a good plan for your life, a plan to prosper you and not to harm you."

BODY LANGUAGE CAN many times say more than your words. There are many physical indications of deception. Be aware of the movements of others, no matter what is coming out of their mouth. God tells us to be "wise as a serpent and gentle as a dove." I believe body language is a powerful way to read between the lines and spot deceit.

DAY 16   January 16

"ALL THINGS ARE possible to those who believe." Deep within your spirit is the ability to walk in faith because God placed it there when he was creating you. Culture works against this faith, but you can call it out anytime you desire and choose to believe, and when you do that, the whole world of possibilities opens up to you. "Only believe."

CONNECT WITH OTHERS, especially if you can fill a need in someone's life. A mother, father, son, daughter, grandparent, wherever there is a loss or a need, step in and be who they need. Life becomes so worthwhile and enriched when you fill the needs in any of these areas. There is such a need for grandmas and grandpas out there. Remember that as you bless others, God will bless you. "Consider others more important than yourself."

Day 17   January 17

A LIFE WITHOUT a dream is like a GPS without a satellite. God gives his people dreams, and it is up to us to go forward and make the dream happen as he gives the knowledge, the provision, and the desire. "God works in us to will and to do his good pleasure." A timely, inspired dream will guide you into the destiny that God has planned for you. Dreams are good, but only if you choose to put action to them. Never give up on your dreams. "In due season, you shall have your reward."

WHEN GOD TELLS us to "consider the poor," it is more than just giving them money. It is encouraging them, praying for them, helping them carry a temporary heavy load, or work with them to stabilize their life and maybe even give them work. "Whatever good you do for the needy, God will do for you."

DAY 18   January 18

THE NUMBER ONE statement in the Old Testament is "fear not," and it appears 365 times—one time for each day of the year. I do not believe this was an accident. It is an order from our Father in heaven! No matter what happens in life, if you remember to look to God and trust God and make a decision to not fear, your life will follow the path that God has set before you, a holy highway that no evil thing may come upon. "Fear not, it will only cause harm."

RESPECT IS THE greatest need a man has, and love is the greatest need a woman has. As our culture strives to undo gender, God has given each gender-specific needs. Just because we think it would be nicer to be another gender does not change our God-given characteristics. Honor and respect the opposite sex and love who God created, both you and them. "God created them in his own image, He created them male and female."

DAY 19 January 19

WHEN YOU CHOOSE to build a spiritual wall around your life, you are building protection for all those within your sphere of influence, a safe place, so to speak, for your family and friends and even for your future inheritors. A spiritual wall is built by living within God's perimeters. Everyone that lives in your life will be blessed, even down "to the tenth generation." What an amazing legacy.

ALWAYS LET INTEGRITY be your guide, and it will direct you down the right path! When you choose to do that which is the "right thing," God is on the same side with you, and you can count on him to rescue you in every situation. Integrity keeps you under God's protective umbrella. If you step out by entering the worldly realm of deceit, greed, and lies, you are setting yourself up for failure. Even little fudges can be disastrous! "Acknowledge God in all your ways, and he will make your paths straight."

DAY 20   January 20

IT IS SAID, "If man does not punish evil, he is commanding it to be done." Apathy is thought to be the appropriate response in the church today, and yet I really believe that if we sit back and do not participate, we are allowing or commanding evil. I am a firm believer that "faith without works is dead," and I believe in prayer, but I believe equally in action!

SOMETIMES WHEN WE ask God to remove a mountain that is in front of us, he does remove it. But other times, the mountain does not move, but he gives us the strength to climb over it. God will always answer your prayers, but it is always on a time schedule that only he knows. Never give up on what you have asked. Stay expectant, but also be willing to climb the mountain that is set before you. "Grow not weary of well doing because, in due season, you shall have your reward."

Day 21   January 21

STOP LOOKING FOR fairness. It will save you a lot of disappointment. Instead, turn your expectations towards your Father in heaven. He is always fair, and he always does exactly what he says he will do. "Has he not said it, and will he not do it?" On the other hand, the world is full of false promises and false hope and disappointment galore. "Those who put their trust in God will never be disappointed."

PSALM 29 SAYS, "The Lord gives his people strength, and he blesses them with peace." Wow! Don't we all just need strength and peace? Remind God of this promise when you feel weak or you're rattled. He tells us to "bring him in remembrance of his Word." You hardly ever hear anybody teach that. So hear me on this one: remind him of what he said, and then believe he will do it. Peace and strength, we got this!

Day 22   January 22

THE ANSWER TO sinfulness is the Grace of God. There is nothing you can do to deserve forgiveness for your sins. Grace is an undeserved gift given to any man who wants to accept and receive it, and it can only be received by faith. When God has his gracious hand upon you, you cannot fail. You may travel through some turbulent times, but you will never fail "because his grace is truly sufficient."

"THOSE WHO EXALT themselves will be humbled, and those who humble themselves will be exalted." Be careful when you think you are above others because God has a way of humbling you. "Don't consider yourself more important than you ought" because just about the time you think you've got it all together, you may find yourself tumbling down. On the other hand, if you truly show humility, God will exalt you.

Day 23   January 23

I HEAR PEOPLE say, "I don't believe in God" Really? Well, what in the heck do you believe in? The world? Science? People? Money? Stuff? What are you going to call on in times of trouble? How can these things help you when you are old and sick and dying? Only "a fool says he does not believe in God." Without God, life is hopeless, and death is even more hopeless. Consider well your choice not to believe.

WHILE WE ARE called to help others carry a temporary heavy load, we are not called to pick up their load. We are all responsible for our own life, and an entitlement spirit is very unhealthy for both codependent participants. Do not get sucked into feeling that you are responsible for others. You are not! Though it is important to help others when you can, your own life is your responsibility!

DAY 24   January 24

LIVE GENEROUSLY AND life will treat you good. When you give, God will give to you. Giving can include many things, from encouragement, touch, acts of service, as well as money and stuff. Purpose in your heart to be a giver because it is truly "more blessed to give than to receive." A giver will always have enough and will always get blessed. Giving is like putting money in the bank. It will take care of you all the days of your life.

ENCOURAGERS WILL ALWAYS be winners. Winners don't trample people down. They encourage others. Anybody can be negative and find fault and criticize and gossip as they point out the failures of others. And sadly, those judgments will come back on those who send them. "Your judgment of people will come back to you in kind." While those who encourage others are the real winners in this world. "Whatever good thing one man does for another, God will do for them."

Day 25   January 25

PSALM 138:8 SAYS, "The Lord will perfect that which concerns me." This scripture is one of those hidden treasures in the Bible. Imagine: anything that concerns you, God is going to perfect it. I don't know about you, but that delights me. Finding these hidden treasures, these beautiful golden nuggets, and applying them to your life is such a blessing and will enhance your life.

ARE THERE PILES of rubble, ash, and junk in your life? Do you feel overwhelmed? Do you feel like giving up? This is a perfect scenario to get a miracle from God. Honor God and trust him for help as you take your first step. "It's not about might, it's not about strength, but by my spirit," says the Lord. Do you have what it takes to overcome? "With men it may be impossible, but with God all things are possible."

DAY 26   January 26

ACKNOWLEDGE THE WEAKNESSES in your life. Be aware of areas where you need a plan when it hits and be realistic when you evaluate your strengths and weaknesses so you can prepare for a logical defense. Know ahead of time how you will handle certain scenarios. Plan your strategy and remember the Lord will fight for you if you stay within the boundaries he has set for your life and do not waiver. "Those who waiver get nothing from God." Stick to your plan!

SOMETIMES WE RACE through life so fast that we miss the little things that make life so sweet. Stop and enjoy the moment! Savor the music of the breeze rustling through the trees, stop and smell the sweet fragrance of a flower, listen to the melodic music of the birds, or make a new friend! Enjoy every moment God has given. Life is fragile. Handle with care. "This is the day the Lord has made; I will rejoice and be glad in it."

Day 27   January 27

THERE ARE MILLIONS of people living in fear! I am amazed at how many people are frightened. Remember "perfect love casts out all fear." "God did not give us a spirit of fear but of power and of love and of a sound well-disciplined mind." If you are operating in fear, be assured "your worst fear will come upon you." Instead, put your trust in God, and you will never be disappointed.

ALL THE CHANGES *in the world, whether for good or for evil, are always brought about by words.* Your words are so powerful, and when they come out of your own mouth, they even have a greater impact on you. When you listen to bad things, it has a negative effect, but when you say negative things, you can set your life on a course of destruction. "The power of life and death is in the tongue." Use this little member wisely.

DAY 28   January 28

OFTENTIMES, WHEN A man thinks he's become wise, he actually becomes a fool. "Don't consider yourself more important than you are ought." Stay humble and remember that when you think you've got it all together, you're on a very slippery slope.

"IT IS GOD who arms me with strength and makes my way perfect." When you ask God, he will give you precise instructions on your future and how your steps should move towards it. The key is to keep your eyes on God and trust him with all your heart and remind him that he promises us "he will direct the steps of the righteous." Strive to be honest, fair, and righteous in all that you do, and this amazing promise belongs to you.

DAY 29 January 29

EVEN WHEN WE serve God well, we ofttimes go our own way without acknowledging him or asking him for direction. I am convinced we will never know until we get to heaven exactly what we have missed here on earth by not following his precise instructions. His Word says, "We cannot even imagine the things God has prepared for those who love him." Serve him well and seek his daily direction.

WE BECOME WHAT we submit ourself too. Watching TV, playing video games, watching the news, all these things are superficial and empty, and to be honest, it is mostly darkness. The language is not edifying, and the games are mostly violent. Instead, submit yourself to God and "keep your mind on the things above not on the things below." Seek out friends who are like-minded and remember "bad company corrupts good behavior."

ONCE YOU REACH your dream, you've got to find a new one. It is important to always have hope for something in the future because that's what keeps us going and keeps us having fun and enjoying life. Faith must have hope to latch on to. Without hope, your faith will be weak, and without faith, we cannot please God. Dream big as you trust God, and always remember to celebrate the partial victories that come along before the dream is fulfilled.

GOD WILL NEVER take everything away from you without leaving you something. Be grateful for whatever you have, and God will bless what you have left not what you have lost. Consider the process of a renovation of an old building. This is how God works in our life. It must be destroyed before it can be rebuilt. Be encouraged, and "keep your eyes on the things above, not on the things below."

Day 31   January 31

GOD PROVIDES THE opportunities, but it is up to us to take advantage of those opportunities. You can't just sit and wait for God to drop pie out of the sky. Keep your eyes open and be aware of the things around you. Be ready to take advantage of opportunities that come your way. "God directs the path of the righteous."

A GOOD TEACHER will lead his student to the threshold of their own understanding. Sometimes "people do not have ears to hear." This means they are not ready to hear certain things, and your time is wasted trying to tell someone something they are not ready to hear. Guide people towards the area where they can receive from you. Find that place you can connect with someone and then gently show them your truth.

February

Day 32	February 1

IF YOU HAVE a need, take that need to God. God can do immeasurably more than you could ever hope or dream for. Ask God for everything, and don't worry that he will say NO because if he doesn't want you to have it, it is because he has something better for you. Ask your Father for everything. "You have not because you ask not." Nothing is too big for God. Trust the gracious hand of God. Odds do not matter if the hand of God is upon you.

A PERSON LIVING for others can and does make a difference. God uses humans to fulfill his plans. Be aware of what is going on around you and allow God to use you to impact others. Share and help others, even if it means stepping out of your comfort zone. And remember "whatever good thing you do for others God will do for you."

DAY 33 February 2

GOD TELLS US, "Do not throw your pearls to swine." Sometimes we waste our time by trying to convince those who refuse to hear. Place your good words in good ground. Do not spend your energy on those who do not want your help or your good words. Be careful because swine can trample you. Pray for those from a distance who do not want to receive your pearls. There are so many good people out there who want your pearls. Save your energy for them and steer clear of the swine.

NEVER LOSE SIGHT of the fact that your decisions and what you do will produce consequences, both good and bad. It is vital to your spiritual growth and well-being that you consider the outcome of choices and actions. A single bad choice can set your life on a course of destruction. "Acknowledge God in all your ways, and he will make your path straight."

AS LONG AS you keep God first, everything else will fall into line. The farther you remove God down the list, the harder your life will be. God tells us, "In this world, you will have trouble." But if you keep God at the helm of your ship, he will navigate you through the troubled waters and turn all those troubles into good. What an amazing promise!

WE HAVE APPROXIMATELY eighty thousand thoughts a day, and it is said that sixty thousand of those thoughts are repetitive. In other words, there are certain subjects that occupy our thoughts daily. God's Word says to "keep your thoughts on the things above and not on the things below." Be intentional as you direct your thoughts to the things of God because what you choose to think about will eventually become your life.

DAY 35   February 4

GOD IS RARELY a God of too much, but he is always a God of enough. The truth is that all of us have way more than we need. Solomon confirms in the book of Ecclesiastes that after he had tried and gotten everything he saw or wanted, it was nothing more than "chasing the wind." Stuff is not the key to happiness. Contentment is the true key to happiness. "Contentment with godliness is great gain."

IMPERFECTIONS CAN BE a gift when you put your trust in God because "in your weakness, God is made strong." Embrace and admit your weakness and give the reins to God. You will be so surprised at what he will do with your tweaks. Believe it or not, your weakness can become your crowning glory.

DAY 36   February 5

WHEN YOU HAVE hit a brick wall and you do not know what to do, when you have reached the end of yourself, you are set up perfectly for a miracle. Throughout the Bible, a miracle only happened when things were a mess. Be encouraged. You are on the verge of a miracle if your faith is in God. "In your weakness, God is made strong." "After you've done all you know to do, stand and believe." But be sure you have done all you know to do first.

"A FOOL'S PROUD talk becomes a rod that beats him." Your mouth can set your life on a course of destruction! Just as a wildfire destroys everything in its path, words foolishly spoken have the same impact. "The words of the wise keep them safe." Be intentional with your words. *It is better to keep your mouth shut and be thought a fool than to open your mouth and remove all doubt.*

Day 37   February 6

NEVER BURN A bridge because you never know when you might have to walk across it again. It is ok to move on from people and things, but it is not wise to take potshots at them as you move on. Always be respectful and leave the door open. "With whatever is within you, be at peace with all men."

IT IS SAID, *For those who believe, no proof is necessary. For those who don't believe, proof is not enough.* When you apply this to the Bible, it becomes even more real because, as a Christian, "we walk by faith not by sight." We don't need physical proof, while unbelievers must have their senses appeased. They need to see it, hear it, or feel it, and even then, they often doubt. It's all about faith, and without faith, no one can please God.

Day 38   February 7

"**MANY ARE THE** afflictions of the righteous. But the LORD delivers him out of them all." Let's face it, afflictions are such a part of life that no one escapes, but God promises those who serve him that he will deliver them. Keep your thoughts on that as you work your way through the perils of the day. "Though there may be tears at night, joy will come in the morning."

ENCOURAGEMENT IS SO important to the human character. We all need encouragement. Purpose in your heart that when you see something pretty or commendable, you are going to verbalize it. So many times, we think something sweet, and yet we withhold the compliment. Don't do that! Remember that when you put perfume on someone else, you will get some of it on yourself. "Whatever good thing that one man does for another, God will do for him."

Day 39   February 8

NEVER LET THE things you want make you forget about the things you have. Our culture is so blessed, and it seems we never get enough. We are so busy hoping and wishing and dreaming about what we want that we often neglect that which we already have. Your gratefulness or the lack thereof about what God has given you will determine what you will get in the end. "He who is faithful with a little will become ruler over much."

ENTRUST AND DEDICATE every single little or big thing in your life to God. Everything that you entrust to him will always be steadfast and solid. Even if it fails, it will open something new. Once you have given it to God, really let it go. He can be trusted, and the peace you get when you really trust God "goes beyond understanding. It is not the peace that the world gives. It is a peace that only God can give."

Day 40   February 9

WHINING AND COMPLAINING will not only separate you from others but will separate you from God. It is a waste of time and energy, and it will reduce you to discouragement, and discouragement is a horrible, dangerous, destructive place to find yourself. Discouragement is usually caused by discontent and destructive bondage. "This is the day the Lord has made; I will rejoice and be glad in it." Always believe something wonderful is about to happen.

"GOD IS HOLY and worthy to be praised." The root definition of the word holy means different. God is different. There is nothing in this earth that can even compare to him. He is omnipresent, omnipotent, and optimal. His love will fill a gaping hole in the heart of every man. A hole that nothing else will fill. A hole created by God for a personal love and communion with his children. "Praise him. He is worthy to be praised."

Day 41   February 10

THERE IS A connection between our thoughts and our behavior. "Cast down wild imaginings and anything that tries to exalt itself above God." Whatever we entertain in our thoughts will eventually manifest itself in the natural world. Replace any negative, ugly, nonproductive thoughts that tries to weasel their way into your mind with whatever is pure, lovely, and of a good report.

GOD SPEAKS TO us continually through sights, sounds, thoughts, impressions, scriptures, and other people. There's no limit to the variety of ways that God can communicate with us. Listen and watch for him in every situation. He is always there, even when it does not appear he is. "Whether you turn to the right or the left, you will hear a voice behind you saying, this is the way; walk in it."

DAY 42   February 11

GET YOUR EYES off the negative things happening in the world today. That negativity is designed to take your eyes off what God is doing. Do you believe the report of the evil news media? Or do you believe God's Word that tells us if we obey God rather than man, we will experience a flourishing finish and we will not be overtaken by the evil that is activated in our country? Keep your eyes on Jesus. In the end, we win!

"THE EYES OF the Lord run to and fro throughout the earth to show himself strong on behalf of those who are loyal to him." When you stand and believe God and his Word, and when you really try to do his bidding, he will show himself strong to you. God will always do what he promises if you do your part, and your part is to simply believe and act on his Word.

Day 43   February 12

PEOPLE ARE ALWAYS going to let you down; this is just part of life. God tells us to handle these disappointments with gentleness. Not with revenge or anger. Sin will always go down in every relationship, whether it be with your family, your mate, or your boss, and how you handle these confrontations will determine the depth of the love that will prevail in your life. "Those who have friends must show themselves friendly." No friends? Check yourself.

IF YOU STUMBLE, make it look like it's part of the dance. That is just the way life should be. If you make a mistake, don't stop and make a big deal out of it, but rather keep moving through life and be willing to laugh at your own clumsiness and admit where you made a mistake. Life is full of mishaps. No need to whine over them, lament over them, or make a big deal over them. It's just the way it is. Choose to "be courageous" no matter the circumstances. You got this!

Day 44   February 13

GOD WILL NOT bless lazy or stingy people. Read that line again: God will not bless lazy or stingy people. "We are blessed according to the work of our hands," and "with whatever measure you give to others, it will be measured back to you." Those are the two scriptures used to base this point upon. You must keep your hands moving and you must be generous to receive God's blessings.

GOD WILL GIVE you "double for your trouble" when you stand in and believe God and his Word. Things will not always flow gently along, even when you are serving God. There will always be trouble in our lives, but if you faithfully hang in there and trust God, you will see a restoration of everything, and God will multiply everything you may have lost. "God will restore the years the canker worms have eaten."

DAY 45   February 14

THE WORLD'S IDEA of love is very different from God's idea. Love is not sex, although that is the icing on the cake—but it is not the cake. Read God's love chapter and then have a blessed Valentine's Day with all those who you love. Happy day!

1 CORINTHIANS 13:4 says, "Love is patient and kind, it does not envy, it does not boast, it is not proud. It is not rude, it is not self-seeking, it is not easily angered, it keeps no records of wrongs, it does not delight in evil, it rejoices with the truth, it always protects, it always trusts, it always hopes, and it always perseveres."

THERE ARE PEOPLE in the world who spend their whole life in low places. Have compassion because we never know when we might end up in the wilderness ourselves. Be sensitive to the valleys and the low places that people are in, and don't be smug about your success. It is wonderful to be proud of where God has brought you, but always remember where you came from. "Be careful when you think you stand, lest you fall." (I hear you, Lord.)

NEVER GIVE UP! If you have been believing God for a long time for something, God is working on it! "There is a time and a season for everything under the sun." Just as an orange on a tree needs a season to sweeten and turn orange, so it is with everything in life. If picked too early, it is sour and bitter. "Grow not weary of well doing because, in due season, you sure have your reward."

"GOD CHOOSES THINGS that are foolishness to the world in order to confound the wise." As you trust God, don't expect the ordinary, boring, and mundane as you travel your life's journey. You never know who or what God might use to rescue and direct you. God is filled with style, drama, excitement, love, and complete sovereignty. I love my Lord.

THERE WILL BE seasons in every life where you will have to do what you feel you are not qualified to do, things that will throw you for a loop, things that will overwhelm you, and yet it is dumped in your lap, and you do not have a choice. When this happens, just embrace it as you acknowledge God and ask him to walk through this trial with you. He promises to put a light on your way and provide a straight path. "I can do all things through Christ who strengthens me." "Be strong and courageous."

Day 48   February 17

REMEMBER THE THREE Rs: *Respect yourself,* *Respect others*, and *take Responsibility* for your own actions. God's Word says to love others as you love yourself, so you won't be able to love others until you learn to love yourself. Be patient with your human frailties, we all have them. Admit your errors, clean up your own messes, and learn from your mistakes. Voila!

DO NOT JUDGE by what you see. Just because someone does not look or even act like a Christian does not prove anything. Only God sees the heart of man, and only God should ever judge a man. "If you judge, you will be judged." Remember what you put out to others is a boomerang that will come back on you. Tread lightly.

"**FAITH COMES BY** hearing the Word of God," and we can damage our faith with what we hear. *Be careful little ears what you hear.* The ear gate is often the way ugly stuff enters into our minds. There are times that we aren't even really listening, and yet we hear things that affect our actions. Guard your ears, especially in these disrespectful days where anything goes. And if you do hear unwanted nonsense, be sure and cast it down.

"**THE FRUIT OF** righteousness is peace." If you are like most men and women, you desire peace more than anything else. Try doing things God's way! Righteousness is simply acknowledging and honoring the Word of God, and with your obedience to God's Word comes the promised gift of peace. "Seek first the kingdom of God and his righteousness, and all other things will be added to you."

DAY 50   February 19

THE NORMAL CHRISTIAN lives in glory! It may not always be easy, but it is glorious, and you will always overcome the trials that life throws at you. "You will go from glory to glory." Life is exciting as your spirit comes alive. The colors are brighter, the flowers smell sweeter, and life is just a joy. Fear is replaced with faith, and darkness becomes light. The heart becomes tender, and life just has a lightness to it. Thank you, Jesus!

WHEN HOPE IS given, reply with action. Move forward proactively as you lean on the hope that God has put in your heart. Don't just sit there and expect pie to fall out of the sky! God says, "After you have done everything you know to do, stand and believe." Do not stand and believe until you have done all you know to do. Get moving!

DAY 51   February 20

MANY WANT SO badly to be "self-made" and in that pursuit, they trample on those who helped along the way to prove their misguided objective. No one is self-made—it's a myth! We are all influenced by someone who has helped to make our life what it is. Always be willing to stop and say thank you to those who have had even a small part in your success. And be sure to thank God as well because ultimately "it is only God who has the ability to give great wealth." And he uses others to help do his bidding.

"FORGET THE FORMER things and do not dwell on the past because I am doing a new thing." Do not define your future by your past. Instead look forward to the things that are ahead and expect God to do "the new thing" he promises to those who believe him. Anticipate a new beginning. Write something new and beautiful on your nice clean slate, keeping your aspirations reasonable with small, sure steps that will solidify the big picture. Be blessed!

Day 52   February 21

TAKE THE TIME to notice the influences around you. Don't wait until later to look back and reminisce about the past and those who have helped you along the way. Pay attention and give credit to those who have encouraged, taught, and even corrected you along your life path. And do not be thin skinned as others try to help you with your journey. Glean from every single person who comes along and remember "the wise man learns by watching, while the fool has to have a rod taken to his back."

YOUR WORDS WILL guide your life, and they will set the direction of your life. Be intentional with your words because they can bring blessing or cursing, and be very careful what you say to yourself. Your words will direct where you go spiritually, emotionally, financially, and in your relationships. Words are so powerful. Be careful who you listen to and what you say. "The power of life and death is on your tongue."

DAY 53   February 22

THE ACCEPTANCE OF Jesus in our life brings us into perfect harmony with God the Father, and with that acceptance comes not only the forgiveness of our sins but also the inheritance of all the promises in the Bible. It sets us on a holy highway that no evil thing may travel on. It frees us to pursue God as a child of the King. When we rightly honor the blood of Jesus, it enables us to "resist the devil, and he will flee." What else do you need?

"'VENGEANCE IS MINE, I will repay,' says the Lord." God will give to people what their actions deserve because he alone knows the human heart. Be at peace as you see the wicked running to and fro, and remember the battle is God's battle. Trust his timing. Justice will be done.

Day 54   February 23

YOUR SUCCESS AFFECTS others around you, and blessings are often contagious. Always be willing to share your booty with your friends and loved ones. There is nothing finer than to see your gifts make a difference in someone else's life. Giving becomes a double blessing, as you get the joy of blessing someone else, and on top of that, "God will do for you what you have done for others."

IF YOU CLOSE your eyes and your ears to the truth of God, you will come to think your carnal ideas and the carnal ideas of the world are accurate. You will begin to call evil good and good evil. This is the natural process of hardening your heart to God, and we can see it everywhere today as our college professors and teachers become more atheistic in their teaching. Remember "the wisdom of man is foolishness to God." Be not deceived. In the end, "every knee shall bow." And as they have sewn, they shall reap!

Day 55   February 24

THE DOORS OF hell are locked from the inside, and those who go there choose to do so. Tread lightly.

NEVER LET YOUR experience determine your faith. Make a choice to believe God's Word no matter what you may see with your eyes. Always choose to believe in the power of the unseen world because "all things are possible to him who believes." Ask God to help your unbelief. We all struggle with unbelief at times, but the victorious will choose to push through as they choose to believe, no matter what. "In due season you will have your reward."

Day 56   February 25

WHEN YOU CHANGE your focus, you change your life. The key is not to get a new house, a different mate, or a better job. The key is to simply change your focus! Magnify God and his promises, and joy, peace, and faith will rise. Magnify your problems, and fear, anxiety, and stress will rise. "Change your focus, change your life!"

WE REMEMBER 10% of what we hear, 50% of what we see, and 90% of what we do. Sometimes the only way we will really get it is to do it! If there is something that scares you, step out and just go for it! Experience is the greatest teacher of all. A college education gives your head knowledge, but you will never be good at what you've learned until you put your learning into practice. "Be a doer of the Word and not just a hearer."

DAY 57   February 26

"I CAN DO all things through Christ who strengthens me." Sometimes God allows things in our lives because "in our weakness, God is made strong." Weaknesses, illnesses, financial problems, relationship problems, and every other trial in our life will fine-tune us and make us better people. Stay on the path though it is steep and windy because it is leading you to your promised land. "Count it all joy when you go to the fiery trials because it is perfecting you" You got this!

YOUR OUTER WORLD reflects your inner world. If everything is outwardly messy and chaotic in your life, that is what's going on in your mind as well. We serve an orderly God, and it is up to you to keep your personal space in order. If you are feeling out of control and your life is a struggle, try cleaning up your surroundings. I guarantee you will feel a whole lot better. "Let all things be done decently and in order." "God is not a God of confusion."

GOD NEVER MADE his laws to punish us. He wrote his laws to help us. Yet every time we choose to sin, we are also choosing to suffer. Every single one of his laws was for our own benefit. I liken it to a parent with their children. The rules in the house are to protect the children from harm. When we go against the rules, we are putting ourselves in danger, and we are removing ourselves from God's protective umbrella.

IF JESUS IS your Lord, you have been given the "keys to the kingdom of heaven," as well as the power to do everything that Jesus did when he walked the earth. Operate in that power as you reach out to help others. Console, encourage, pray, touch, heal. Be bold with the things of God as you walk out your life. This life is a flash in the pan, and only what's done for God will last. All else is nothing more than chasing the wind!

DAY 59   February 28

BEING PART OF God's family has nothing to do with DNA or religion, but rather it is spiritual. It is about the heart, and only God can know your heart. He knows your heart even better than you do. He sees past everything you say or do and only sees you by your heart. We may be able to fool other people, and we can even fool ourselves, but we cannot fool God. "God knows the secrets of the heart."

IF YOU WILL commit to keeping a smile on your face, it has been proven to make you happier. A smile causes your brain to release happy endorphins. Giving thanks, being happy, and putting a smile on your face can change your life. "Give thanks in everything." "Whether you abase or whether you abound, be grateful."

March

WISDOM IS OFTEN found in strange places. And more times than not, it is found in failure. Failure is never really a failure if you learn from your mistake. I honestly think the most successful people in the world are those who failed and yet got up and tried again. "Count it all joy when you go through the fiery trials because it is perfecting you.

"THERE IS WISDOM in many counselors," but you still need the right voices to bring the right choices into your life. Show me your friends, and I will show you your future. Your friends are a photograph of your future. "Where there is no council, the work fails, but in the multitude of counselors, there is safety." When you choose to remove the voice of God, you will begin to hear other voices. "There's a way that seems right, but in the end, it brings destruction." stick with God and godly friends.

DAY 61   March 2

PEOPLE WHO ENGAGE in drama will usually try to drag other people into their drama. Steer clear of radically dramatic people because they will jack with your peace and make you miserable. Dramatic people are usually bored and trying to get attention. Don't get sucked into their drama. "We are called to a life of peace."

RELATIONAL STRESS CAN wreak havoc and wreck your life. Circumstantial stress will weaken your life. God tells us to "be anxious for nothing, but in all things, with prayer and supplication, make your requests be known to God, and the peace that passes all understanding will guard your heart and your mind through Christ Jesus." Worry and anxiety can kill you! Worry is worthless. It dishonors God, and it is actually functional atheism. Tell God what you need and then put your trust in him.

DAY 62   March 3

WHEN YOU INCREASE your connection to God, things of the world become strangely dim. The farther away from God you get, the bigger your problems get. "Draw close to God, and he will draw close to you." He is not going to invade your life unless you ask him. If your spiritual engine is not running, it will coast for a while, but eventually it is going to crash and burn! One day, your haphazard lifestyle will catch up with you. We do not get by with anything! "God will judge everything, even what is done in secret. The good and the evil."

NEVER DOUBT THAT God can do miracles! He can make the deaf man hear, he can bring sight to the blind man, he can raise the dead, and he can walk on water. Why would you doubt he can fix your puny problems? The only part you need to play in a miracle is to "believe."

DAY 63   March 4

APOLOGIES COST YOU nothing, and yet they can produce a bountiful harvest. Be the first to try to make things right with someone who you have been at odds with, and a blessing will surely befall you. It doesn't matter who was right or wrong. In fact, if you make the first move and you were the one who was right, the blessing is even bigger. God loves a peacemaker. "With whatever is within you, be at peace with all men."

THERE ARE MANY people in our culture who do not think they need God, but I guarantee you the day will come when every single human being needs God. When one finds himself in a place of danger, they will always turn to God. Everyone needs God, and "one day, every knee shall bow." Every single human being will have to answer to God, whether they believe in him or not.

Day 64   March 5

"CHANGE IS ALWAYS a part of every life, so don't plan too far ahead. Wake up every day with an expectancy as you do what you have to do and do it well. God will direct your steps as you are diligent with the things at hand. Don't spend too much time planning your days ahead. A better idea is to savor the day and do the best you can with what you have, leaving space for God to interject new things that are "above and beyond anything you could ever hope or dream for."

WE CAN'T ALWAYS choose what happens to us, but we can choose how we respond to what happens. When we put our trust in God, we can rest assured that no matter what happens, it will work towards good for us. The peace that comes from knowing you are in God's hands cannot be bought with anything the world can offer. Walk out each day, one day at a time. Every day has its own set of problems. Concern yourself with the issues of today, and don't fret over tomorrow. "Fret not, it will only cause harm."

Day 65   March 6

I HAVE HEARD it said that you are only as sick as your secrets. It is so dangerous to keep things in. The Word says, "Confess your sins one to the other, that you might be healed." The Catholic Church offers "confession," and although I am not Catholic, I approve of this. However, a trusted, godly friend can be equally as effective. We should never be doing anything we don't want people to know.

ASK THE LORD to lead you and guide you to the company that he wants you to minister to because you can have a lot to give to someone, but if they are not ready to receive it, you will be wasting your talents. The wrong people can feed your own doubts and insecurities back to you, so it is imperative you surround yourself with at least two or three like-minded people who can confirm what God is trying to say to you and do through you. "As iron sharpens iron, so a man sharpens the countenance of his friend."

DAY 66   March 7

THERE IS ALWAYS a gap between what God tells you to do and what you see and feel. This is a God-ordained gap. Hold on because God will close the gap. Following God is purely a faith walk. If you can see something, that is not faith because "faith is the things hoped for but not yet seen." When you choose to walk in faith, anything is possible. Get out of God's way and trust him. "Those who put their faith in God will never be disappointed."

DELAY DOES NOT always mean denial. God's timing is different than our timing. And God will increase your faith while you wait! You have to be willing to wait and believe in order to receive from God. Ask, believe, and wait! This is the key. I dare you to quote out loud that you will believe God and then be willing to wait and believe that God will do what he promises. "Has he not said it, and will he not do it?"

DAY 67   March 8

THE WORD HUMILITY means to stay low. "Never consider yourself more important than you ought." If you want to get high in your life, you have to get low in your heart first. Spend your days thinking about and doing for others. A self-serving person will eventually crash and burn. When pride and selfishness come, then comes disgrace. Do not let pride, arrogance, or selfishness sneak into your life. It is the ultimate destroyer of success. "Consider others more important than yourself."

DO NOT ALLOW your past to cripple your future. If Jesus is your Lord, your past cannot hinder you. Forget about your past and look to your future. Your past is real, and there may be mistakes and sins in your past, but God promises he has forgiven your past and set a beautiful future before you. "Keep your eyes on the things ahead and not on the things behind."

CONFIDENCE AND NEGATIVITY are polar opposites. Negativity is a choice, and you cannot have what God has for you if you're negative. Be selective in your thoughts, and do not let negativity take you down. Surround yourself with positive people and be one of those who helps others to see the good in everything. Good is always there if you choose to see it. "In the dark and meanest things, there always, always something sings."

GOD WILL INTERRUPT you and offer help. God does reach out to people, and he often reaches out through other people. God will see you in your trouble and offer help. Unfortunately, many times we reject the hand that God uses to help, and more times than not, this rejection is rooted in either pride or unbelief, and both of these things will block God. God will never force himself on you, but he will always offer a hand. Take it.

MICAH 6:8 SAYS, "O people, the LORD has told you what is good, and this is what he requires of you: to do what is right, to love mercy, and to walk humbly with your God." I love the simplicity of this God-given mandate. It sounds pretty simple, doesn't it?

WHEN FEAR AND doubt is faced, put your faith in God. Who are you listening to and believing? The voice you listen to should be the Lord's. When you hear things from others or even from your own head that is contrary to anything the Lord says, cast it down. Never let negative, condemning words make a nest in your hair. Replace all negative thoughts with the powerful Word of God. "The Word will not come back void." It cuts through everything.

Day 70   March 11

THE RIGHTEOUS CRY out, and the LORD hears and delivers them out of all their troubles. "The LORD is near to those who have a broken heart and saves such as have a contrite spirit." If you are dealing with problems that just never seem to go away, have you really cried out to God? I mean really cried out to God! Not just whine and complain but actually cry out to God. Because if you haven't, you're missing the boat. "Has he not said it, and will he not do it?"

ANGER IS A natural response, and it can be effective as long as you keep God in the equation and do not let your temper rage. "A hot-tempered man stirs up strife." Anger is often what motivates people to make changes in cultures, schools, and homes. God used anger and outrage throughout the Bible to make changes, and it is only when the anger turns into a perverted anger that is twisted and violent that anger is not good. Righteous anger is totally acceptable, as long as it is kept in check.

DAY 71   March 12

WHEN STRENGTH IS lacking, respond with trust. When you put your trust in God, he will always come through for you. "In your weakness, God is made strong." God wants to see you through to victory. Take your best shot, and God will finish it for you, but you have to take the first step. Acknowledge God as you move forward, and God will guide, protect, and bring you to success. "Acknowledge God in all your ways, and he will make your path straight."

GENEROSITY UNLEASHES THE power of God! If you choose to give with a cheerful heart, I promise your "little" will become much! God will always increase what you give. If you hoard your money and stuff, you will never have enough, and your wealth will bring sorrow. Purpose in your heart today to become a giver and watch the power of God come alive in your life.

Day 72   March 13

IT IS NOT what you do for God that really counts. It's more why and how you do it. There are lots of people physically serving God, but way too often, it is for their own glory. "All the glory and all the honor must go to God." Remember God only looks at the heart. Think about that. You can be doing all the wonderful things in the world, but if you're not doing them for the right reasons, you are sowing into the wind.

WHEN YOU FEEL like you've done everything you know to do, and you feel like you cannot deal with that same problem that's been tormenting you for so long, you are almost to the end. Because "when you have done everything that you know to do, then stand and believe." In the Greek, that means to abide in God and to let him do everything. The rest is up to God. Be encouraged.

DAY 73   March 14

IF YOUR MAP tells you to turn right, and you decide to turn left, this does not negate your direction, but rather it takes you another longer way to get to where God wants you to go. God promises us he will direct our path, but you need to ask, trust, and obey. When you feel that nagging check in your spirit, stop and reevaluate your direction. Remember "God works in us to will and to do his good pleasure." You'll know which way to go.

A HARD HEART has a darkened mind and is excluded from the life of God. They are earthbound and live in the futility of their own mind. What an awful place to find yourself. God tells us to "renew our mind." And this can only be done by a conscious decision to read, believe, and live our life according to the Bible. Life is hopeless and futile without God. Choose today to renew your mind. "God is always there to answer those who call unto him."

Day 74 March 15

REACH OUT TO God, and he can do a miracle in your life. Whatever is withered or deformed or tweaked in your life, if you will reach out to God, he will restore it. Never sit and whine about the things that are wrong in your life if you have not bothered to ask God to help. Call out to him. "Draw close to him, he will draw close to you." It's up to you to reach out and ask. "You have not because you ask not."

GOD PLAYS A very significant role in the favor you see in your life. God is orchestrating the parts of your life you could've never done on your own. There is a certain element where only God can make things happen. God will help you engage with powers outside of your own capabilities when you totally submit your life and your belongings to him. There is nothing sweeter than the taste of God in your life. "Taste and see that the Lord is good. Blessed is he who takes refuge in him."

DAY 75   March 16

WHEN CRISIS HITS, it is normal and natural to feel anxiety, worry, hopelessness, anger, bitterness, and helplessness. These are the natural response of man, but when these things try to shake your confidence, remember to latch on to your faith and remember the promises of God. "Draw near to God," and this will bring him on the scene. And with him on the scene, you will get a grip on all the fears that try to overwhelm you. Thank you, Lord!

"EVERYTHING IS PURE to those whose hearts are pure. But nothing is pure to those who are corrupt and unbelieving because their minds and consciences are corrupted." If you find yourself being suspicious or negative or entertaining bad thoughts, you need to press into God and let him overhaul your thought process. God tells us how to think in Phil 4:8, and I encourage you to stop, read, and apply his instruction. "And now, dear brothers and sisters, one final thing. Fix your thoughts on what is true, and honorable, and right, and pure, and lovely, and admirable. Think about things that are excellent and worthy of praise."

Day 76   March 17

"**GOD MAKES A** way where there seems to be no way." God is bigger than the circumstances, and he is still in charge, no matter how things look. Trust him and press into him. We are experiencing things that are prophesied in the Bible, and God has a good plan for those who look to him. "Fear not, it will only cause harm." If you have never called out to Jesus, this would be a good time. It is as simple as saying, "Help me, Jesus." Keep your faith and remember "those who put their trust in God will never be disappointed."

ALL GOD ASKS of us is that "we do what is right, we love mercy, and we walk humbly before him." I think we should be able to pull that off. Always make good choices and do the things that you know are right, show mercy to others by being considerate, tolerant, and forgiving, and remember to be humble before the Almighty God. We got this!

DAY 77   March 18

LEARN TO BE content no matter what situation you find yourself in. Whether you abase or whether you abound, make a decision to pursue contentment. This does not mean you just sit back and do nothing to make things better. But it does mean that "after you have done all you know to do, trust God for everything else." And choose to be content with what you have and where you are. Contentment is a twin to gratefulness, and this combination will open the windows of heaven in your life.

NEGATIVITY IN ANY personality will squirt cortisol into your brain and cause you to be wary, depressed, and angry. It will put people into a negative state of mind. Cortisol is a stimulant and is addicting, as are all stimulants. Steer clear of negative talk and do not allow it to proceed out of your mouth. No one is exempt to the toxins that negativity spews into your whole system. "Whatever is pure, lovely, or of a good report, think on these things."

Day 78   March 19

IN ORDER TO be really happy, you must be grateful. When you choose to see the good in everything and learn to thank God even for the trials that cause you to grow, life will be a delight. Remember you will always find what you are looking for. "In the mud and scum of things, there always, always something sings!" Watch for what sings, even in the dark and meanest places.

"WHAT SORROW AWAITS those who argue with their creator." We are living in a time of arrogant lawlessness. A time where educated people think they know more than God as they openly spew blasphemy out of their mouths and call evil good and good evil. But be not deceived. God is not mocked. Stand firm on the Word of God because every dot, dash, and tittle of it is true, and a day is coming when every single knee will bend. Our God reigns!

NEVER BELIEVE IT is too late for you or anyone else. It is never too late! It is not how you begin your life, but rather how you finish, that establishes your legacy. If you ain't dead, you isn't done. It is not too late! Get a grip on hope. Find people who encourage and spur you on as you steer clear of those who discourage you. We are to love everyone, but choose close friends who celebrate and encourage you. "As iron sharpens iron, so the countenance of a friend sharpens a friend." "Spur one another on to love and good works."

WE CAN DRAW the presence of God in our life by believing him. Faith draws God to those who trust his Word. A power descends upon those who choose to believe. When God's presence invades your life, you will see miracles because you will have eyes to see and ears to hear. There comes with your choice a deep-down confidence and "peace that goes beyond understanding, not like the world gives, but only like God can give."

DAY 80   March 21

THOUGHTS ARE POWERFUL, and God tells us "to cast down wild imaginings and everything that exalts itself above the Word of God." Every action starts as a thought. "As a man thinks, so he is." Don't allow your mind to focus on anything that is negative, or unclean, but rather be intentional where your mind wanders because the body will always follow where the mind goes.

MANIPULATION OF ALL kinds is nothing short of witchcraft. I often see Christian women manipulating their husbands, and it is very grievous. A woman of noble character looks to God and does not need to manipulate her husband or anyone else to get what she wants. Even subliminal manipulation is completely out of order. This is not God's best for us, and we will never find total joy until we do things God's way. "Make your requests be known to God, and the peace that passes all understanding will guard your heart and your mind through Christ Jesus."

DAY 81   March 22

"**WE CAN MAKE** our plans, but the Lord determines our steps." It is good to have a vision and to move towards it, but be prepared for changes that may block your way. God promises he will direct our steps, and they may be different from your plans. Trust that detours are part of his divine plan for you. While it is important to be determined, there is a fine line between determined and stubborn. "Acknowledge God in all your ways and lean not on your own understanding, and he will make your paths straight."

NEVER EXALT YOURSELF or anyone else above God, or division will happen. We serve a jealous God! When you put things above God, you are taking a chance that they will be removed from your life. The very first commandment that God gave us was "love God with all your heart and all your soul and all your mind and put no other God before me." When we obey this one commandment, everything else falls in line. We love you, Lord.

DAY 82   March 23

"GRACE IS SUFFICIENT." Grace will always provide an escape route for you. Grace does not always spare you from the trials, but grace will always take you through the trials. When grace is in your life, it doesn't mean you won't go through the fiery trials. It just means that "no weapon formed against you will prosper." The weapons will still be formed against you, but they cannot prosper when his hand and grace is upon you.

"GOD'S POWER IS incomparable to those who believe." If you are a believer, ask God today for your greatest need. This does not mean a new Cadillac or great riches, although he may choose to do that for you. It means what do you really need? If you can "only believe," God will honor your prayer. Remember it may not be the way you thought or in the timing you planned, but if you do not waiver, you will have whatsoever you believe, for "God is not a man that he should lie. Has he not said it, and will he not do it? Or has he said it and not made it good?"

DAY 83   March 24

GOD TELLS US to repent and believe. We all know what it means to believe, but what does repentance really mean? Repentance is to change one's mind, although it is quite deeper than we think changing our mind is. The basic meaning is really to change your purpose, your perceptions, and to basically change your life. It is putting your trust in Jesus, as you realize you are a sinner and you need the grace of God. It is a true sorrow for what you have done wrong in life. And after that, he says, "Only believe."

AS PRAISES GO up, deliverance comes down. When we praise God, even in the midst of trials, we are opening ourselves up to the blessings of God. God's Word says, "Praise for the spirit of heaviness." Praise will lift depression, oppression, and heaviness right off you. Never just sit and wallow in pain, but rather sing and praise the Lord. "There may be tears at night, but joy will come in the morning."

DAY 84   March 25

GOD WILL ALWAYS keep his promises, but he will not keep your potential. That is up to you. It is our responsibility to take the promises and our potential to bring those promises to pass in our life. We have to use the Word as a weapon to bring about the promises. "It is written." God puts things in our heart, but we do not automatically step into it. We have to seize those promises.

THE WORD GRACE is described as unmerited favor. And yet I would assert it is much more than that because the Word says Jesus walked in mercy and grace. If the word grace meant unmerited, it would not be used when referring to Jesus. Grace is the empowering presence of God within you and enables you to become the person God intended you to be. Ask God to fill you with his grace. "I can do all things through Christ who strengthens me."

Day 85   March 26

ALWAYS MAKE THE choice to do what is right. If you always do the right thing—even when things are wrong—in the end, everything will turn out right. It is so easy to rationalize and defend our self-serving, self-protective choices, but I believe we were all created with an innate knowledge of right and wrong, and when we choose "right," we are choosing God! And when we "choose God and his righteousness, all other things will be added to us."

AS LONG AS you keep God first, everything else will fall into line. The farther you remove God down the list, the harder your life will be. God tells us that "in this world, you will have trouble." But if you keep God at the helm of your ship, he will navigate you through the troubled waters, and turn all those troubles into good. What an amazing promise!

Day 86   March 27

LISTEN TO PEOPLE with curiosity and wonder. Most times, we listen with half an ear as we plan how we are going to respond. We are more interested in what we are saying rather than listening and learning from others. Determine in your heart to be an intentional listener. "Consider others more important than yourself."

NEVER GIVE UP! If you have been believing God for a long time for something, God is working on it! "There is a time and a season for everything under the sun." Just as an orange needs a season to sweeten and turn orange, so it is with everything in life. If picked too early, it is sour and bitter. "Grow not weary of well doing because, in due season, you shall have your reward."

DAY 87   March 28

NO MATTER HOW many times you fall in life, keep getting back up! There are tons of hurdles along your life path, and some of them will be impossible to gracefully hurdle over, and sometimes you will even fall to the ground, but always get back up and press your way forward. "Run your race as if to win." Finish your race for the upward call on your life.

"WHATEVER YOU RESIST will persist." If you have an issue of error in your life, never defend it because you will never be rid of this negative issue until you are willing to embrace it and admit your error. It is so childish to defend something you know is wrong. The sooner you admit your error, the sooner you will be free from it. "He who loves discipline loves knowledge, but he who hates correction is stupid."

Day 88 March 29

GOD WILL OFTEN deepen your roots so he can strengthen your limbs, which will eventually sprout leaves and blossoms that progress into beautiful ripe fruit that will be distributed in due season to those in your sphere of influence. Don't try to rush the season of ripening. "There is a time and a season for everything under the sun." Enjoy the season of growth and soak up the Word that is the fertilizer that causes this beautiful process to take place.

OUR GOD CAN and will take the crooked places in your life and make them straight, and incredibly, those crooked places will become your strength because "it is in your weakness that God is made strong." Give your life and all your tweaks over to God. He can make you into who he intended you to be.

DAY 89   March 30

THE FIRST MISTAKE can be an accident, but the second time it's usually a choice. It is said that to keep doing things the same way over and over and expecting things to be different is nothing short of insanity. Mistakes can work towards good for us when we learn from them, but if we continue to make the same stupid mistake over and over—insanity! "The wise man learns by watching, while the fool has to have a rod taken to his back."

TRUTH AND LIES will always be out there. God promises us to direct our path and lead us along paths of peace, joy, and contentment. Every truth will always line up with the Word of God. It will be established by two or three witnesses, it will be peaceful, and God will confirm it in your heart. "Test the spirits" as you always check with God about lies and truth. God promises "everything done in the dark will come to light."

DAY 90   March 31

LOVE CAN OFTEN cause pain, and this does not necessarily mean the relationship is not from God. "No pain, no gain." True love that has a depth ofttimes goes through lots of trouble as well as many adjustments, and many times people are so quick to abandon a relationship because there are issues involved. True love will work through these issues, and in the end, "the iron that has been through the fire is the strongest."

THERE ARE PEOPLE in the world who spend their whole life in low places. Have compassion because we never know when we might end up in the wilderness ourselves. Be sensitive to the valleys and the low places people are in, and don't be smug about your success. It is wonderful to be proud of where God has brought you, but always remember where you came from. "Be careful when you think you stand, lest you fall."

April

YOU WILL NEVER know God through worldly, scholastic knowledge. Worldly people will never understand the things of God. It will appear as foolishness to them. They are actually blinded to God's Word. God does this because he has given the keys to the kingdom of heaven to those who believe. These bright, educated people do not even have the ability to understand, until they choose to believe. I often hear people say, "Are they blind?" Yep, they are. Be patient. This is God's battle, not yours. Your part is to love them and pray for them.

TRY NEW THINGS in your life! Lots of people don't like change, but I guarantee you, those people who are not willing to learn and make changes will end up old, boring, and bored. Life is filled with wonderful, amazing journeys, sites, people, smells, etc. Be intentional about experiencing life to its fullest. Remember the word mediocre means halfway between success and failure. Never choose mediocrity! "Run your race as if to win."

DAY 92   April 2

"WEEPING MAY ENDURE for a night, but joy will come in the morning." Always remember God promises that sorrow, pain, grief, and all things negative are temporary. When you are in the throes of pain of any kind, comfort yourself with this wonderful promise. God's promises are powerful for those who believe. Train you mind to look to God when you need help. "God draws near to those who draw near to him."

DO NOT ALLOW others to make a mess in your life or in your spiritual space. Guard, secure, and fortify yourself, always keeping in mind that "we are called to a life of peace." Do not submit to anyone or anything that jacks with this coveted gift. Gird up your mind and rest your hope fully on the grace of God. Separate yourself as much as possible from those who stir up chaos in your life.

DAY 93   April 3

"**GOD WILL NOT** withhold any good thing from those who do what is right." We serve a good God. We serve a God who wants us to prosper and be in good health. When we choose to walk in integrity and honor God's principles, we will see "the goodness of Lord in the land of the living." Circumstances should never be able to shake your trust in the goodness of God. "You will be like a tree planted by the water that nothing will shake." Hang on to that amazing promise.

PURSUE WHAT IS good and right and be done with selfish ambition and exploitation because, in the end, the only thing that really matters is what's done for God. If you wake up the next day and you feel bad about something, you know it is wrong for you. If you continue doing things that you know are wrong and it is causing guilt, you are playing with fire. Life is so sweet and so precious when everything you do is unto the Lord.

Day 94   April 4

IF YOU STILL struggle with unforgiveness, you have not truly grasped the forgiveness of God. He has mercifully poured out his grace and mercy upon all mankind and forgives all who ask! He tells us we are forgiven as we forgive. Remember God knows exactly what happened to you, and he understands, and he will help you if you ask him. But if you choose not to forgive others, God will not forgive you.

THERE ARE TIMES that a believer needs to fight for what is right, but God's Word says to "fight the good fight of faith." Your faith can actually win a battle, it can change hearts, it can open doors and move mountains. Couple your faith with proactive prayer and you can beat any opponent! Your faith brings God on the scene in your life to make the correction and see justice done. You will never be defeated if you keep yourself in the presence of God.

DAY 95   April 5

ANY FOOL CAN criticize, condemn, and complain, but it takes character to be understanding and forgiving. And besides that, God says, "Fret not, it will only cause harm," so when you fret over things, they will actually get worse. Train yourself to look on the bright side of things. I don't know about you, but I avoid complainers and whiners like the plague. People like to deal with positive people, and this will eventually compute into a successful life.

AS A CHRISTIAN, "you are blessed to see the things that you see." Many times, the unsaved are unable to see the truth. They are actually blinded, and many of the mysteries of God are not revealed to them. In fact, oftimes they find the things of God to be foolish. Do not judge the unsaved for their blindness, they really cannot see truth. Be respectful and kind because "it is God's loving kindness working through you that will draw them in."

DAY 96   April 6

THERE WILL BE negative issues in our life that we will have to learn to live with. It could be spiritual, emotional, financial, physical, or relationships, but the key is to ask God for his mercy and grace to cover you as you walk out this life with all its problems. The Scriptures say, "His grace is sufficient." In other words, we can handle anything if we have God's grace. I like it and I'm going for it! Grace, Lord, grace!

WE ARE CALLED to set ourselves apart from the ways of the world. Our culture hops into bed with anyone, they accept all sorts of things that are offensive to God. And we have developed a seared thought pattern. This is not alright with God, and even though it may seem sweet and God's ways may seem rigid, we have got to do things God's way no matter how the world thinks or what they may say about us. We are God's ambassador, and his ways are the only way.

Day 97   April 7

HOW YOU DO anything is how you do everything. If you are unfaithful in the little things, you will be unfaithful in the big things as well. God knows who will be faithful, and he gives accordingly. When you are slothful or haphazard, you are shooting yourself in the foot! It will cause you to limp through life wondering why you never seem to get anywhere. "Whatever you do, work at it with all your heart as if you're working for the Lord." "If you're faithful with a little, you will become ruler over much."

INTERRUPTIONS IN OUR life are usually God moving you towards the plans he has for you. We get so busy doing our own thing and making our own independent plans that God has to interrupt us! Never throw a fit over interruptions because you never know what God is saving you from. Be willing to gently flow with life and think of it as a journey. "In their hearts men make their plans, but it is God who establishes their steps.

WAITING ON GOD is often hard because everything in our culture is right before us, and we want to take things into our own hands and make things happen. God calls us to wait on him. There is always a period of waiting between a calling and a fulfillment of God's calling. Just because you are positive about your calling does not mean it is immediate. You will have to wait. "Those who wait on the Lord shall renew their strength. They shall rise up with wings like eagles, they shall run and not grow weary." Slow down and wait on God!

"GOD HAS BLESSED us with every possible spiritual blessing." Inheritance is a big deal, and notice that his promise is spiritual not necessarily financial. God predestines us to move towards the calling that he has planned for us because he knows who will believe and trust him even before we are born. Remember every good and perfect gift is from above. Trust God as you seek your unique calling.

Day 99   April 9

RESERVE YOUR OUTRAGE for special occasions, like "righteous anger." Today, outrage is a way of life. Everyone is outraged about something. The news, social media, politics, everywhere we look, people are angry, insulted, or outraged. "The anger of man will never accomplish the purposes of God." Let's purpose in our hearts to not participate in this nonproductive lifestyle. When you let anger get control, your life will always get worse. Many times, we try to fight what is "God's battle."

WHILE WE ARE called to help others carry a temporary heavy load, we are not called to pick up their load. We are all responsible for our own life, and an entitlement spirit is very unhealthy for both the codependent participants. Do not get sucked into feeling that you are responsible for others. You are not! Though it is important to help others when you can, your own life is your responsibility!

DAY 100   April 10

LIFE IS NOT always a mountaintop experience; it is filled with both mountaintops as well as valleys. Most times, it takes a journey through a valley to reach the mountaintop. Never resent these necessary valleys, but travel through them as best you can as you acknowledge God as he guides you through. No matter how treacherous the journey, there is a light at the end. Stay the course because "though there may be tears at night, joy will come in the morning."

"EVEN A FOOL is considered wise if he holds his peace." Sometimes the less said, the better! The mouth can either bless or it can curse. It can build up or it can tear down. It is a powerful little weapon, and it should be used with caution. Words spoken have a tremendous impact, and we all need to be more intentional with what comes out of our mouths because our words can actually set our life on a course of destruction. Sometimes the best thing you can do is "shut up!"

Day 101 April 11

ISAIAH 43:1 SAYS, "I have called you by name." God knew your name even before you were born. He knows absolutely everything about you. And he will never leave you or forsake you. Abandonment issues is one of the most painful conditions of both animals and humans, and all of us will experience that feeling of abandonment at one time or another in our life as our loved ones die or choose to separate themselves from us. But the good news is that "God will never leave you or forsake you." He is the only one who will walk this entire journey with you. Thank you, Lord!

THE WRATH OF God rests on those who choose to live separate from him. Wrath is actually a curse, and it is the exact opposite of a blessing. God's Word says, "I lay before you life and death, blessing and cursing, choose life." Therefore, we are always living under one or the other, and it is our choice. I choose life. I hope you do too!

Day 102   April 12

YOUR FEELINGS CAN block God's blessings quicker than anything else, and if you don't learn this, you'll never walk in God's victory. Feelings, at best, are fickle! We are not supposed to live our lives according to how we feel or think. We are supposed to live it by always doing what is right. Feelings do not always tell the truth, and what you think is not always correct. Live your life by always doing what is right, even if it feels wrong.

THE ONLY TIME you will ever grow spiritually is when you do something that you really don't want to do. It's so easy to do everything that you do well, but growth will prevail when you do things that are out of your comfort zone. Just as you will never get more muscle unless you lift a heavier weight, spiritual growth will be stunted if you don't expand into new, uncomfortable territory. "I can do all things through Christ who strengthens me."

DAY 103   April 13

AT ONE TIME in history, the church was not called Christian but was called "The Way," in reference to living the right way. The way that shows others the correct way to live. There are some who will never step a foot in church, and we will be their only example of the church. We live in a very dark world. Let your light shine. "Live your life in such a way that no man can say evil of you."

GOD WILL NEVER use you to get revenge! God will see justice done; this is not your responsibility. Show restraint when you have the urge to retaliate or get revenge. If you choose to fight with the arm of the flesh, you may lose. But when you let God handle it, he will always see justice done. God loves justice. He tells us to "pray for those who mistreat us." Do it God's way! It always works.

Day 104   April 14

WHAT GOD DOES for you is not based on who you are, how handsome you are, how much money you have, or how many Hail Marys you say everyday. God loves you no matter what your record or your status might be. His love is unmerited by you and is offered to every single living human being. He never rejects men, but many reject him. You can go to hell, but it will be your choice. "Choose life."

IF THERE IS secret sin in your life, there will eventually be public exposure because "whatever is done in the dark will someday come to light." Secret sin is the most dangerous sin of all. It is deadly, and it will eventually kill you! Confess your sins to a trusted friend, pastor, or priest. Because "if you confess your sins, God is faithful to forgive." Light will always dispel darkness, just as a small candle will light up a whole room.

DAY 105   April 15

SEED TIME AND harvest is how God works in the world. It is true in every aspect of life, and like growing a garden goes, so goes everything under the sun. Plant your garden of life as if to harvest whatever you plant. You cannot plant corn and get watermelon. Whatever you plant you will harvest. Friends for friends, love for love, good for good, and so on. "Be not deceived, whatever you sow, you will reap."

"OH, THE DEPTH of the riches and wisdom and knowledge of God!" That scripture just delights me. God's depth is more than the human mind can even grasp. His wisdom is beyond anything that man could ever conjure up. When you come to the place of truly knowing this, the peace that goes beyond understanding will overtake you. There is honestly nothing sweeter than to be able to say, "I really, really believe this." Nothing can shake your faith at that point, and that kind of faith can move mountains. And that, my friends, is where I am. Thank you, Jesus, and yippee!

Day 106   April 16

FALSE IDOLS STILL exist, though not in the form of molten images. Television, cell phones, the internet, food, astrology, your family, and anything else that you put your trust in. False idols are often very appealing and look innocent. But beware because, in the end, they bite like a snake. We serve a jealous God. "Love him with all your might and all your strength."

GOD'S GRACE IS given freely to all who accept it. You can never be good enough to earn the grace and mercy of God. It is only his grace that allows you to have communion with him. We could never achieve this by our works because God is pure perfection and man is not capable of perfection. But God in his mercy sent Jesus to take all our transgressions on himself, and our part is to accept this magnificent gift and "only believe." Wow.

Day 107   April 17

STUDIES HAVE PROVEN sheep respond to their shepherd's voice. They will not respond to the call of strangers, but when their shepherd calls, they go towards his voice. It is much the same with God and his children. We can hear our shepherd. It is that "still quiet voice that says, 'Stop, go this way.'" It is that gentle urging to do what is right, it is that calm assurance that all is well with your soul. Listen for the good shepherd's voice and choose to follow it all the days of your life. Have a wonderful, fun, happy, blessed Easter.

OUR SIN FILLS us with darkness. And as a result of our sin, we become separated from God. And every human commits some sort of sin every single day. The average human heart believes they can get to heaven just by being good. Yet even on our best day, we as human beings cannot be good enough. God provided Jesus as an advocate for our sins. Take the time to accept this wonderful gift that not only saves your soul but will change your life. Have a completely blessed Easter Sunday.

DAY 108   April 18

MONEY WILL MULTIPLY everything in your life. Money is not evil, but "the love of money is evil." While money can make life easier, it can also create tons of problems, especially when it is looked to as a God. It creates an accumulation of everything, and with that accumulation comes a myriad of problems. More divorces are caused by money than any other reason. Money tends to make people feel they do not need God. This is why the Bible says, "It is easier for a camel to go through the eye of a needle than for a rich man to get to heaven." Be sure you are ready for this tricky commodity before you ask for it.

EVERY SINGLE THING that happened in our life is leading us to where we are at this moment. Many have taken the long way around, but you are still here. If you have trusted God, then he has directed your steps and brought you to this moment in time. "Acknowledge God in all your ways, and he will direct your path." Keep your eyes on the road ahead and continue your journey knowing "God has a good plan for your life."

DAY 109   April 19

WHEN YOU FEEL thankful inside, you need to show your gratefulness on the outside. Gratefulness should not just be a heart thing, but it should also be a tangible outward expression that witnesses to others. A good way to show gratefulness is to "pay it forward." If God has blessed you, pay your thankfulness forward by doing something active to help someone else. "Whatever good thing one man does for another, God will do for him." If you need help in your own life, do something for someone else!

IT IS SAID that "whomever is happy will make others happy also." Isn't it just the truth! Don't you just love to be around happy people? Life can be so full of trials. and yet those who carry their load lightly and have a zest for living can lift others up. Living happy is both an art and a discipline. Choose to be that person who brings a light into every room you enter, that one who chooses to see the good in everyone and everything, that one who expects everything to turn out fine. It is your choice, you know.

Day 110 April 20

EVEN THOUGH GOD has predestined you, you still have to make the choice to follow his predestination. Your choices can change the good plan God has for you. When you choose to follow God, you can rest assured there is a good plan set for your life and you can calmly travel your chosen path with the confidence that all is working towards good. Hallelujah!

UNDERSTANDING GOD'S TIMING is one of the mysterious keys to success. "There is a time and a season for everything under the sun." And just as we cannot force the fruit to ripen any faster than God's timing, we cannot force things that are not quite ready. Always be willing to wait on God as you continue to move forward doing what you know to do until the time of harvest has come. "Grow not weary of well doing because, in due season, you shall have your reward."

DAY 111   April 21

"BE STRONG AND courageous." Courage makes all the other attributes possible. Courage does not happen by chance because God says "BE" strong and courageous, implying it is a choice. Being courageous does not mean fear is not present. In fact I believe that most courageous actions happen during intense times of fear. Make a choice that you are going to be strong and courageous under every circumstance in your life. "I can do all things through Christ who strengthens me." You got this!

FAITH ISN'T TO believe long and far into the misty future. It's simply taking God at his Word and taking the next step. Faith begins where man's power ends. Every man is given the same measure of faith, and just like a muscle, it gets bigger and stronger with use. Exercise your faith daily by believing God for the little things, and then when faith is needed to believe for the big things, you will be ready.

DAY 112   April 22

WHEN WE SEE a need and we have the means to help, we should always lift a hand. While it is good to just pray for someone, we should always be willing to do something in the physical realm that needs to be done. When we pray for someone, God searches for those who will help him answer that prayer. Let him use you to help others. And remember that when you help others, God will help you in your time of need. "Whatever good thing one man does for another, God will do for him."

THE MOST SIGNIFICANT sign you are a part of God's kingdom is that when you sin, you do not have peace. While it is great to read the Bible, go to church, and memorize scripture, nothing compares to the conviction of God to recognize your need for God. Do not ignore conviction, but rather recognize it and ask for forgiveness. God always responds to a "help me" prayer from his children.

Day 113   April 23

"SOW A THOUGHT, reap an action. Sew an action, reap a habit. Sew a habit, reap a destiny." This is the process that takes place to form your success or the lack thereof. Remember everything begins as a thought. And every action has a consequence, whether it be a good action or a bad action. Determine to set your life on a course of success by keeping "your thoughts on the things above, not on the things below." Create good habits that will change your destiny.

BLESSINGS FROM GOD are always spiritual, even though sometimes it will include physical blessings. If the blessings always meant "physical," then it would eliminate many poor countries and people. It is always spiritual first and physical second. Never believe that just because someone is poor, they are not blessed. In fact God's Word says, "Blessed are the poor because they are rich in faith." Many times, physical blessings are a hindrance to faith. "Never despise small beginnings.

DAY 114   April 24

SOMETIMES WHEN WE pray, God will answer immediately, while other times, we have to wait as he walks us through the fire. But he always hears your prayer, and he always answers, even though it may not be as you expected. God's timing is a mystery that our puny human mind will never understand. Trust and believe. "Those who wait on the Lord shall renew their strength, they shall rise up with wings like eagles, they shall run and not grow weary, they shall walk and not faint."

FAITH IS THE bridge that will carry you over the rivers of hopelessness. Faith is the thing that offers hope, and faith is a choice. We are all given a measure of faith at birth, and it is our responsibility to nourish it by reading God's Word and choosing to believe it. Even when things seem impossible, choose to stand on what God says. Putting your complete trust in what God's Word says will change your life. "Taste and see that the Lord is good."

Day 115 April 25

YOU CANNOT HAVE faith if you do not have hope. A lack of hope will discourage, depress, and actually make you sick and shorten your life. "Hope deferred makes the heart sick." The Word tells us to "stir up our own self." Whatever it takes to keep you stirred up is your responsibility! Who you hang out with, what you read, what you watch, and what you say can all affect your hope. Purpose in your heart to stir yourself up and share your hope with others.

"YOUR BODY IS a temple of the Holy Spirit." Take better care of yourself! Try to imagine the windows of a church all broken out and the grass up to your knees and weeds everywhere. This is a picture of what you look like when you choose not to take care of your body, both physically and outwardly. Your whole being represents our Lord, and just as a rundown church would not draw people to it, the same goes for you. Always look your best and do it as unto the Lord.

DAY 116 April 26

NEVER LOSE SIGHT of the fact that your decisions and what you do will produce consequences, both good and bad. It is vital to your spiritual growth and well-being that you consider the outcome of choices and actions. A single bad choice can set your life on a course of destruction. "Acknowledge God in all your ways, and he will make your path straight."

GOD GAVE MAN dominion over everything on earth, and he created man in his image. "God created man upright, but man has devised many schemes." All the ugly, unnatural things that are going on were all devised, planned, and acted out by mankind. None of this is done by God, although I often hear people say, "Why would God allow this to happen, or why would he do this to me?" Not God, folks! "All good things are from above." Old Red Ears and the fallen man get the blame for everything else. If it's not good, it's not God.

DAY 117   April 27

"WHOEVER WALKS WITH the wise becomes wise, but the companion of fools will suffer harm." This warning is from the book of Proverbs. Proverbs is full of wise sayings, and if you take the time to study it and apply it, wisdom will abound in your life. Never think that you are above the influence of a bad companion. If God tells us to beware of something, we need to take heed. Surround yourself with wise companions, and you will find yourself acting accordingly.

SIN IS AN uncomfortable subject, and it thrives in darkness and isolation. "Confess your sins one to the other that you might be healed." Do not protect or rationalize your sin. And do not deny that you are a sinner because we are all sinners! Sin is not just an "oops." It is a serious offense against God and yourself. Admit and confess your sins because a repentant heart is completely forgiven, and "God does not even remember your sin anymore."

GOD HAS CALLED each of us to do a particular thing. You cannot do everything, and don't even try, or you will miss your calling. God has placed you in a particular place, and he tells us to "occupy the land." Your sphere of influence is your calling. There are some that get called to other places, and of course they should go. But generally speaking, your calling is right before you. Think of every person you meet as a divine appointment. Be sensitive to the spirit of God as he directs you. "My sheep hear my voice."

OUR GOD CAN and will take the crooked places in your life and make them straight, and incredibly, those crooked places ofttimes become the highlights of your life because "it is in your weakness that God is made strong." It is in those weaknesses that when you call out to God, he will take your tweaks and rework them. "He is the potter, and we are the clay."

DAY 119   April 29

THE DNA OF the Lord is always persistent, and even though we may give up on people and things, God never gives up on us. God speaks to everyone differently, so don't expect the directive someone else got from God will come to you in exactly the same way. God speaks to you in a language that you will understand. "You are fearfully and wonderfully made."

MANY TIMES, WHEN people have done us wrong and it pushes us into another part of life because of their wrongdoing, it is actually God moving you somewhere. Stop and look at any situation in your life where you feel that someone has done you wrong. Check the circumstances and pay close attention to where God has brought you because of that negative situation in your life. Sometimes God is using someone in a negative way in order to get you where he wants you to be. "The steps of the righteous are ordered by the Lord."

DAY 120   April 30

JOY IS MAGNIFIED by a nightmare! We all know that feeling of waking up from a nightmare and being so grateful it was only a dream. That is an example of the joy that comes after the trials are over. In the midst of your trials, keep yourself encouraged by reminding yourself of God's promises and believing that no matter what happens to you, it will work towards good if you love God and are called according to his purpose for you. "There may be tears at night, but joy will come in the morning."

"GOD WILL NEVER look on wickedness with favor." God is holy, and he will never come onto the presence of sin. "There cannot be darkness where there is light." You cannot keep one foot in the world and expect God to protect you from its pitfalls. God does not operate in the things of the world. The world is completely contrary to the kingdom of God. The beautiful part of this is that you get to choose.

May

LET THE WORD of God adjust your life, and do not try to adjust the Word of God to fit your life. When you know what the Word says and you choose to go against his Word, "you are trampling underfoot the blood of Jesus." And without the blood of Jesus, there is no sacrifice that can help you. God will always forgive you, but sin takes you out of God's protective covering, and there is always a negative consequence to every sin. Stay under his protection by believing and obeying the laws that he has set before us.

"LOVE THE LORD your God with all your heart and soul and all your might and don't put any false idols above him." This is the very first commandment. And one of only two left after Jesus died on the cross. Jesus said all the commandments were fulfilled in "love your neighbor as yourself" and "love the Lord with all your heart." If we can make a conscious effort to live our life with these two commandments we will fulfill the commandments of God in all their fullness.

THE BIBLICAL DEFINITION of contentment is so important to know. Contentment is not based on money, people, your situation, or stuff. True contentment has to do with your understanding and acceptance of our Savior. Everything else is temporary and requires more and more to maintain. Jesus is enough. I know that sounds crazy, but when you really, really know who your Savior is, the things of earth become strangely dim. Praise God!

EVERY MAN HAS flaws in his character, but do not accept these flaws as just being who you are! Recognize and manage your character flaws. To deny them and defend them not only allows them to operate at peak capacity, but it is downright stupid and can destroy relationships. Never defend your flesh when it is out of order. Take charge of your personality and ask God to help you. Remember "God is faithful to finish the work that he has started in you," but you have to do your part to help.

DAY 123 May 3

CONCERN IS ACCEPTABLE, but God tells us not to fret or worry. In fact, he says, "Fret not, it will only cause harm." Fretting makes things worse! Pray about everything and take your concerns to God. Petition him by thinking out loud and talking to God about your concerns. Prayer does not have to be eloquent or lengthy. It just has to be a sincere conversation with God as you work out your concerns. Prayer works.

GOD WILL BRING grace and acceptance right in the middle of your mess if you look to him. We serve a gracious God who will give you grace and forgiveness over and over and over! You may give up on him and others may give up on you, but God will never give up on us. "Where sin abounds, much more so does grace." Even when you are a mess, God still loves you. Stay with him. "He's got a plan, and it's a good plan."

DAY 124   May 4

FAITH IS THE bridge that will carry you over the rivers of hopelessness. Faith is the thing that offers hope, and faith is a choice. We are all given a measure of faith at birth, and it is our responsibility to nourish it by reading God's Word and choosing to believe it. Even when things seem impossible, choose to stand on what God says. Putting your complete trust in what God's Word says will change your life. "Taste and see that the Lord is good."

A BITTER HEART is way worse than a physical injury! The key to a successful life is not what happens to you but rather how you handle what happens to you. We have all seen people who have had incredible physical injuries and yet they continue to joyfully participate in life. Then there are those who become bitter, and even though their body is whole, they wither away. "Happy is he who puts his hope in the Lord." No matter what your lot in life, "rejoice, again, I say rejoice."

DAY 125   May 5

BOREDOM IS A lack of wonder, and the older we get, the more it takes to fill our hearts with wonder. When we are young, the world is our oyster. We believe in pie in the sky and pink elephants, but as we mature, the luster of the world begins to dull. Solomon said, "It is all chasing the wind." In the end, when your eyes grow dim and your body begins to ache, the only real wonder in the world is God. The magic of serving God never grows dull. Keep yourself stirred up as you think of the miracles he has done in your life, and then watch for the treasures he strews along the path of those who expect it.

"YOU WILL SHOW me the way of life, granting me the joy of your presence and the pleasures of living with you forever." I love that scripture. Ask God to show you the way of life that he has for you and choose to walk in the joy and peace that he promises those who seek him. We are living in a time of great turmoil, and there is no other way to truly find peace than to walk along the holy highway that he has prepared for those who love him.

Day 126   May 6

MANY TIMES, VICTORY requires defeat, and most times, you have to lose physically to gain spiritually. "No pain no gain," as the story goes. When something is removed from your life, something else will always take its place. A loss means a gain! Be cognizant of the new things that God replaces the old things with. Sometimes we get so busy lamenting over what we've lost that we don't even see what we have gained. "Forget those things that are behind and look towards those things that are ahead."

THE WORD SUFFER or struggle is in the King James Version of the Bible 165 times. We always want to run away from struggles, but we have to go through the hard part before we can get to the good part. A lot of our suffering is connected to how we choose to respond to it. Struggles are just a part of life, "and this too shall pass."

Day 127   May 7

"THE STEPS OF a person are established by God." Though God directs our steps, he also partners with us to do "his good pleasure." God will work with us to fight the giants and part the deep waters in our life, as he gives us the desire to follow the path that he has set before us. If you trust him, he will lead you where you are supposed to be. Though the path may twist and turn, stay the course. "He has a good plan for your life, a plan to prosper you and not to harm you."

NEVER LET THE things you want minimize the things you have. The grass is not greener on the other side! Be intentional about deciding to love the things that are yours. As you love and care for that which is your lot in life, it will cause it to prosper and increase. Keep your little plot of life weeded, watered, and fluffed up, and it will produce a harvest. "Be faithful with a little, and you will get a lot."

DAY 128   May 8

PSALM 27:10 SAYS, "Even if your mother and father forsake you, I will take you up and love you." We all know there is no love like the love of your mother and father, but on this Mother's Day, always remember our Father in heaven loves you even more than they do or did. Revel in this thought as you celebrate Mother's Day.

MOTHERS, THERE IS no greater joy nor greater reward than to be given the awesome responsibility of loving, teaching, and coming along side another human being. A chance to know how to love unconditionally. A chance to learn how to be selfless as you give up your own comforts. And as the years go by, you find that you have a loyal, lifelong friend, confidante, and even a care-taker if needed. The most important career you could ever embark upon is the rearing of these precious people God has entrusted to you. Sending a special prayer of hope to every mother. I pray your day is blessed with an abundance of family love and that you are surrounded with all the things that make you happy.

Day 129   May 9

"WORK OUT YOUR own salvation with fear and trembling." It is our responsibility to "study to make yourself approved." I often hear people say things about the Bible and God that are completely untrue. I honestly feel it is dangerous to not know the truth about our God and our book of instructions. Just as you cannot be a doctor without studying and doing your homework, the same is true for your life and your eternity. "Study to make yourself approved."

ALL OF US have been given a special group of eight to fifteen people who God has strategically placed in our life. Recognize and acknowledge these unique people and learn from them as they learn from you. Many times, these people are only here for a temporary lesson, while others walk your life journey with you. "As iron sharpens iron, so the countenance of a friend sharpens a friend."

DAY 130   May 10

IF GOD IS with you and you face your trials based on faith, you will always win. I don't know about you, but I find that so comforting. If you look to God as your Lord, and you really trust him, every step you take is guided by his hand. He promises the steps of the righteous are ordered by him, implying that even a wrong step will be a right step as he guides you along your path. Faith is all that is required to receive this amazing promise from God. "Only believe."

GOD IS OUR captain, not just a coach or our partner. He is omnipotent, all powerful, the creator of all things. Turn your life and all its particulars over to him if you want maximum success. You can muddle through life and maybe even bumble into a few successes, but you will never reach your maximum potential until you put God into his rightful place in your life. "Those who put their trust in God will never be disappointed."

Day 131   May 11

I CONSIDER MYSELF to be the "queen of little." My personal life scripture has always been "if you're faithful with a little, you will get a lot." This has proven to be true in my own life, and next to honoring God, I consider it to be the single most important thing that helped me to achieve success. It wasn't my brilliance or my good looks. And I sure didn't have much money, but what I did have, I was faithful with. And it grew into a beautiful garden that harvests daily. "Those who are faithful with little will become ruler over much." Thank you, Lord.

THERE IS NO reason we cannot be happy and joyful, even in the midst of intense problems. Because the Word says, "How blessed is the man whose transgressions are forgiven." If you are a child of God and Jesus is your Lord, this promise is yours! Blessings will follow you all the days of your life. Will this remove all problems? No, but you will be blessed and joyful right smack in the middle of negativity. Yippee!

Day 132   May 12

"**BE ANXIOUS FOR** nothing, but in all things, with prayer and supplication, make your request be made known to God, and the peace that passes all understanding will guard your heart and your mind through Christ Jesus." I love that promise! He tells us not to be anxious about anything! He gives us explicit instructions in this scripture about how to overcome worry: prayer and supplication. Put the same energy and time towards prayer that you are putting towards worry, and I promise your life will change.

NEVER TAKE YOUR own revenge. Leave room for the Lord! God will always see that justice is done, and he sees the whole picture, while you only see a small picture. "Pray for those who mistreat you," and let God do the judging. If you try to fight your own battles, you will probably lose. Do not retaliate when insulted or threaten revenge, but rather leave your case in the hands of God who always judges fairly.

DAY 133   May 13

SOMETIMES THERE'S NOTHING left to do but to suck it up and go on. There are times in your life that you just don't need to talk about things anymore. What's done is done. There is nothing more annoying than someone who whines over and over how sorry they are about something. They actually keep the misdeed alive. State the error, either yours or someone else's, say you're sorry or forgive those involved, and be done with it. We all make mistakes. "Forget those things that are behind, and move towards those things that are ahead."

THE THINGS OF the world will never satisfy you. In fact, you will crave more and more as you look for satisfaction. This is exactly how drugs, pornography, greed, and alcohol take control over people. There is nothing in this world that can satisfy that God-shaped void in your life. Nothing else will work. "The joy of the Lord is your strength."

Day 134   May 14

FLESH AND BLOOD will never be able to explain to you who Jesus is. In fact, the puny human mind cannot grasp on its own this incredible, miraculous story. Only the spirit of God can reveal the truth about who Jesus is. Understanding and choosing to believe is necessary to receive the gift of salvation. "Believe in your heart and confess with your mouth that Jesus is Lord, and you will be saved." If you are not sure who Jesus is, ask God to reveal the truth to you. "You have not because you ask not."

FUTURE VISION IS believing God has good things ahead. No matter how much bad news you have gotten, God still has a good plan for your life. You will be constricted by fears in the same way you are fueled by your faith and inspired by hope. Stir yourself up with hope, and trust that what God has promised, he will fulfill. "Has he not said it, and will he not do it?"

DAY 135   May 15

GOD IS IMMENSE, he's huge, omnipotent, relentless, and very unusual. He rarely does things as you expect. "His ways are higher than your ways, and his thoughts are higher than your thoughts." Expect God to show up, but don't expect God to do things the way you would expect. Instead, expect surprises and remember God is in everything.

ANYTHING THAT YOU keep hidden will always keep you in bondage, and you will never be healed. You have to get things out to get over them. "Confess your sins one to the other that you might be healed." God can take your pain and turn it into gain. Secrets are dangerous. Secrets keep you in prison. If you don't feel like you have anyone you could talk to, sit in a chair and speak to your Father in heaven out loud and tell him your secret. He already knows them, but speaking them out loud to him is very healing.

DAY 136   May 16

WHATEVER IS GOING on in your mind is what will be going on in your life. Be aware of your thoughts and your words because they determine your progress. And remember empty thoughts can be just as bad as negative thoughts. "Empty space is a place" and leaves room for any whim that presents itself. Fill your mind with the Word of God and "cast down all wild imaginings that try to exult itself above the Word of God." Replace any negative thought that comes into your mind with a positive confession from the Word of God.

IF SOMEONE HURT you ten years ago, do not allow that hurt to continue hurting you today. If you know the Lord, you are not a victim! The victim mentality is a turnoff. Get over it! We all have issues, and we all have people who have mistreated or abused us, but to continue to allow the past to hinder your present is totally unproductive. "Forget the things that are behind and move towards the things that are ahead."

Day 137   May 17

THERE ARE THOSE who I call the good ole boys. Those who believe they can do things their own way and they will still get to heaven. Good ole boys usually lead a decent life, but a decent life is not the requirement for entrance into heaven. "Believe in your heart and confess with your mouth that Jesus is Lord, and you will be saved." That's the truth of it, folks.

IT IS NEVER God who rejects people, but on the contrary, it is people rejecting God. Even those who say they believe in him often ignore him. I believe that if people really knew the value of serving God, they would be shocked. God will pass over millions of people to bless the one person who believes and trusts him. "Taste and see that the Lord is good. Blessed is he who takes refuge in him."

DAY 138   May 18

RESPECT CANNOT BE given. It has to be earned. We earn respect! We cannot act like a jerk and expect people to respect us. We can make a conscious effort to love everyone, but respect is not so easily given, and once respect is broken, it is hard to regain. Respect is shown through actions as well as words. When we choose to throw hateful, mean, nasty words around, we are creating an ugly environment that is not only felt by everyone nearby but is also contagious! Steer clear of disrespectful, foul-mouthed people. "Be not deceived, bad company corrupts good behavior."

THE WRATH OF God is not what people want to hear or talk about. The theological understanding of wrath can change your perspective of God because God is so holy, and he must handle the things that are out of order. The fullness of God's wrath is a passionate, emotional response to the things that are not right. Thank God for his wrath because that is what keeps the world from being overrun with sin.

Day 139   May 19

"**GOD IS THE** light of the world, but many people prefer the darkness." This seems ridiculous, yet it is the truth. Many in our culture have hardened their hearts and love the darkness. They call "evil good and good evil." Note how the church is being persecuted. Note how Hollywood portrays Christians as weirdos and even diabolical. Do not be drawn into the darkness. Stay in the light, and God will direct your steps as he keeps you from stumbling.

THERE IS A preparation to receive the presence of God when you purpose in your heart to serve others. God will give you insight on how to help others. "But to each one is given the manifestation of the spirit for the common good." Share yourself and your gifts with others because that is why God has blessed you. You are blessed to be a blessing.

Day 140   May 20

YOUR SPIRIT IS where you get a conviction from God, and if you are living in such a way that you are offending your spirit, you are blocking the voice of God. Your spirit is actually your conscience, and we know instinctively when we are saying things we should not be saying or when we are behaving in a way that is offensive to God. It is dangerous to ignore your conscience because it is what God gave us to keep us out of trouble. "You will hear a voice behind you that says stop, go this way." Listen to it!

IF YOU KEEP your mind on yourself and rarely associate with others, you are flirting with danger. You are putting yourself in a dark little box that is void of learning. You stagnate in that little box, as you focus on your own limited knowledge over and over and dwell on your own problems. "A wise man learns by watching, while a fool has to have a rod taken to his back." Always stay open to learning, and remember "there is wisdom in many counselors."

Day 141   May 21

BEING STEADFAST IS a wonderful attribute, but there can be a fine line between steadfast and stubborn. And stubborn will rob you of growth. Every time I hear someone say, "I have always done it this way," or "This has always worked for me," I know this person is not teachable. The world is ever-changing, and while I appreciate the old tried and true ways of doing things, we need to remain teachable all the days of our life. "There is wisdom in many counselors."

IF GOD SAYS to do something a certain way, we need to follow his precise instructions, much like following a map. If you are supposed to turn left and you choose to turn right, you will not get where you planned to go. Oh, you will get somewhere, but you will miss the bullseye. Directions must be followed to a tee to hit the mark. If God says it, we need to do it! "Has he not said it, and will he not do it?"

DAY 142   May 22

SULKING IS IMMATURE, ungodly, and extremely selfish. Tucking your tail between your legs and running is never the proper way to handle the situation. Although sometimes a quiet time can bring productive thoughts and a calming down, the quiet time should not be spent rationalizing why you were right and the other person was wrong. A fair analysis is to admit your part in the problem and make the needed correction from your end. It always takes two to tango! "We are called to a life of peace." Do your part to maintain that peace.

SO MANY TIMES, we miss the obvious by looking way out there somewhere for something sensational. More times than not, what you are looking for is right under your nose! Within your own sphere of influence lies your strength to affect the world. It is not usually way out there, and the people within that sphere are your people. Scour your world and watch for God's direction. "I will give you every place where you set your foot."

Day 143   May 23

ANGER AND UNFORGIVENESS not only makes your spirit wither but it makes you physically ugly! If you just take a look at the face of someone who is angry, they never look pretty or handsome. Anger is an acid that will eat you from the inside out. I don't care what people have done to you. Get over it for your own sake. Always remember that God says, "If you don't forgive others, he will not forgive you." Holding anger against someone doesn't hurt them, but it sure hurts you. Let it go!

POSITIVE IS NOT positive until we know the negative. If life were always good, I guarantee you we would not know how to appreciate it. It is only in the opposition that the positive becomes so powerful. He tells us to rejoice in our sufferings because it is perfecting us. And besides that, "God is made strong in our weakness."

PSALM 37:4 SAYS, "Delight yourself in the Lord and he will give you the desires of your heart." Tell God what you want and then get on with it and do not continually remind him over and over about the desires of your heart. He knows what your needs are, and when you truly serve him and give him your time and your life, I guarantee he will give you back the things that your heart desires. This is one of my favorite promises.

FIRST THINGS FIRST. "Seek first the kingdom of God and his righteousness, and all other things shall be added unto you." Focus on God. Worry will not add one good thing to your life. In fact, it will only cause harm. "Keep your eyes on the things above and not on the things below." When you choose to seek God, you will find all the other stuff you have been whining about will fall into place.

Day 145   May 25

WHEN WE CONTEMPLATE on God's Word, we will prosper, be blessed, and have "good success." The more time you spend in the Word of God, the better success you will have. I guarantee you that if you will soak up God's Word and act on what he says, even if it doesn't make sense to you, you will walk in the good life that God has planned for you. Jesus said, "I wish above all things that you would prosper and be in good health even as your soul prospers." God wants you successful and healthy!

IT IS EXCITING and fun to serve God! It opens your life to miracles! And furthermore, when you are really serving God, you will be making good choices, and good choices just make life sweeter. Life is never boring. There is always an element of excitement and anticipation of what God might do next. If you haven't made the choice to ask Jesus into your heart, may I ask why?

Day 146   May 26

WHAT IS GOING on in your life is usually what is going on in your mind. Thoughts produce attitude. The Word says, "Guard your heart with all diligence because out of it flows the issues of life." The heart and the mind are associated! Bad thoughts and mental habits will form your life. You can never get beyond your own thoughts. If your thoughts are negative and lousy, you're going to have a negative and lousy life. Change your thoughts, change your life.

GRATITUDE CAN BE a perfect prayer that will bring about miracles in your life. Gratitude represents the purest kind of faith, and sometimes actual words are not even necessary. The actions displayed by a grateful heart can be even more powerful than any words. God loves a grateful heart. "Give thanks to the Lord with a grateful heart because his faithfulness is everlasting."

Day 147   May 27

"GOD'S WORD NEVER returns void." It will always accomplish what he sends it to do. If you have found a promise and you have been standing on that promise, it will produce! It will not be as you thought because his ways are higher than your ways. Be expectant and prepared to accept your promise in a new and different way. His Word will accomplish its purpose.

OUR LIFE IS like a poem that is written by God himself. When you choose to follow God, there is a plan laid out for you that is ordained. There is a perfect plan, and it does include trials, but it also includes amazing, exciting, and wonderful miracles. Get hold of that thought and trust that as you walk out your life, God walks beside you and directs your steps, and whatever does come against you, "God will work towards good." Even the bad will turn good.

Day 148 May 28

JUST BECAUSE YOUR prayer is not answered at once does not mean God has said no. God has a timing process that must be filled. God's timing is not like our timing. "To God, a thousand years is like a day and a day is like a thousand years." If you have prayed and asked God for something that is within his realm of "right," then you can rest assured that unless he has something better for you, "in due season you shall have your reward."

SIN IS NEVER without consequences. God always forgives you when you ask, but this does not remove the consequences. There are many things in our life that can never be fixed! You may have to live with the devastation that your sins have caused, but God can and will work things towards good to those who love him and look to him. Embrace and accept where your sins have brought you, and then, "only believe."

Day 149   May 29

IF JESUS IS your Lord, you have been given the "keys to the kingdom of heaven" as well as the power to do everything that Jesus did when he walked the earth. Operate in that power as you reach out to help others. Console, encourage, pray, touch, heal. Be bold with the things of God as you walk out your life. This life is a flash in the pan, and only what's done for God will last. All else is nothing more than chasing the wind!

I WOULD RATHER have you like me than love me. It is much easier to love someone than to like them. We are told to love everyone, but "like" is a personal choice. Sometimes we just flat-out do not like someone, and it is OK as long as you are respectful and kind. You do not have to associate with those you do not like. "Love others as you love yourself," and spend your days with those you like.

DAY 150   May 30

"**WHEN YOU WALK** with the wise, you grow wise. But the companion of fools suffers harm." Your friends have a huge impact on your growth in life. "Be not deceived, bad company corrupts good behavior." Be kind to everyone, but choose your friends wisely because their persona will rub off on you.

WHEN YOU FEEL like you've done everything you know to do and you feel like you cannot deal with that same problem that's been tormenting you for so long, you are almost to the end. Because when you've done everything you know to do, God will do the rest. After you've done every single thing you know to do, then "stand and believe." In the Greek, that means to abide in God and to let him do everything. Do not stand until you have done everything you know to do!

DAY 151   May 31

YOUR LIFE IS not falling apart. It's falling into place. Sometimes things have to get worse before they get better. I compare it to pruning a tree. The tree looks pitiful when it is being pruned and the branches are being lopped off, and then there is a season while it may appear it is dormant, but then it springs new life, and it's more beautiful than ever. Pruning and purging is necessary for new growth. Such is life. "There is a time and a season for everything under the sun."

WHEN GOD MAKES a promise, he will perform it! Men may break promises, but God will NEVER break a promise. "Has he not said it, and will he not do it?" "He is not a man that he should lie." Find the promises of God in the Bible and believe them! Your belief activates those incredible promises that are scattered throughout the living Word of God. "Study to make yourself approved."

June

GOD'S WAYS ARE higher than our ways, and when things seem like they are a mess, it is often God at work in our life as he positions us for better things. When we don't understand God, we often resist things that we perceive as bad, and it wears us out. Embrace your situation as you remind yourself that just because something feels bad, it isn't necessarily bad for you. Learn to trust God even when your circumstances are hard to understand. "Those who put their trust in God will never be disappointed."

THE CHOICE OF blessing or cursing in your life is up to you. And incredibly, those "blessings and cursings come down even to the tenth generation." It seems like everyone would choose blessing, but unfortunately, they don't. Anytime an individual chooses to step outside of Gods protective perimeters, they are setting themselves and possibly their offspring up to be potentially cursed. "I lay before you life and death, blessing and cursing. Choose life." You know what to do. Do it!

DAY 153   June 2

RELATIONSHIPS HELP YOU overcome the troubles in your life. "It is not good for man to be alone because he has no one to pick him up if he falls." Stay in fellowship because it is proven that people stay younger, happier, and healthier when they are in close fellowship with others. This doesn't mean you have to be married; you could have fellowship with like-minded friends. The old saying that says *a problem shared is half a problem, and a joy shared is twice a joy* is absolutely true. And remember, "those who have friends must show themselves friendly." It is up to you to make and keep friends.

"DOES IT REALLY matter?" should always be asked before choosing to pick a fight in a relationship. Some things just should be ignored. You cannot change others by bickering and sulking, and negativity will kill relationships quicker than anything else. God says, "It is God's loving kindness working through you that will draw them to repentance," not your negative, know-it-all, judgmental, uncompromising attitude. Be kind!

DAY 154   June 3

"TWO ARE BETTER than one because they have a good reward for their work." While it is wonderful to be capable and self-sufficient, God's Word says, "It is not good for man to be alone." Friends and family should always be part of your day. Do not choose to do life alone. Share your burdens with others as you help others carry their burdens. "A burden shared is half a burden, and a joy shared is twice a joy."

"FAITH SHOWS THE reality of what we hope for; it is the evidence of things we cannot see." And it is impossible to please God without faith because, when you exhibit faith, you are recognizing God's existence. A life without faith is hopeless, and even those who do not believe in God will recognize their need for faith in something as they turn their trust towards false gods. There is only one true God. Serve him because "all else is futile and chasing the wind."

DAY 155   June 4

HEALTHY RELATIONSHIPS SHOULD have the freedom to disagree without negativity. Disagreement can be a stimulating factor in a union. Adaptability is a must for good long-term relationships. Even the best of relationships will have some difference of opinions. How you choose to adapt to the differences in your relationships will determine your success thereof. "Those who have friends must show themselves friendly."

CONFUSION IS A combination of worry and fear, and confusion is never from God. "God gives us a sound, well-disciplined mind." Confusion is caused by a lack of trust in God. "Fret not, it will only cause harm." Let the clarity of God's Word permeate your mind and do not allow the confusion and chaos that runs rampant in the world affect you. "Those who keep their mind on Christ will have perfect peace."

Day 156   June 5

WHEN PEOPLE SEE others blessed, ofttimes they try to keep them down. The fallen-man syndrome is usually not happy for you when you do good. Do not be surprised if others, even your friends, try to sabotage your success. Look to God rather than men for approval. The rare friend will really applaud you when you outdo them in any area. Try to be one of those rare friends who encourages the success of others. "Rejoice with those who rejoice and mourn with those who mourn."

BE DETERMINED TO be happy in life. And it is not about money and stuff either, it is about choosing to be happy inside. There will always be ugly stuff and ugly people to deal with, and if you allow these criteria to determine your happiness, you will waiver and be unstable in all your ways. Decide to be happy! Not because of people, stuff, the weather, your finances, or even your health but because God and his promises are the source of your joy! "Seek ye first the kingdom of God, and his righteousness and all other things shall be added unto you."

Day 157   June 6

YOU WILL NEVER harvest what you do not plant. If you want love, you have to plant love. If you want joy, you have to plant joy. You cannot plant corn and expect to harvest watermelon. What you give, you will receive. If you are stingy with life, life will be stingy with you. "Give and it shall be given unto you. Pressed down, shaken together, and running over shall men give unto you."

GOD WILL NOT bless something outside of what he allows. If you have been praying and believing for something and have not gotten an answer to your prayer, consider that you might be praying outside of God's boundaries. In our world today, there are many things accepted as normal, and yet they are not accepted in God's kingdom. Be sure you are praying and believing for something God would honor because "the effectual fervent prayer of a righteous man avails much." If it is not availing much, something is wrong.

Day 158   June 7

ALL ROADS DO not lead to heaven! Oh, it sounds good, alright, but we serve an omnipotent God who gives very specific instructions on what road leads to heaven. The Bible is "the absolute truth," and it is the only absolute truth! And it is the only sure way to heaven. "Narrow and straight is the path to heaven, and few will go on it, while wide and easy is the path to destruction, and many will follow it." Which path have you chosen?

WHEN YOU SPEAK it, you activate it. "The power of life and death in the tongue." Use your tongue to speak to those ugly things that are in your life. Every time you say something negative about yourself or the things in your life, you are activating power in that area! We have the power to trample on serpents and scorpions, and there is a threat that is being formed against our country that is enormous. Speak audibly, out loud, to those things that you see. Use the name of Jesus against them. Your words are arrows that go out and pierce the enemy.

DAY 159   June 8

GOD WILL OFTEN teach people in the extreme. I compare it to riding a horse. You put the bit in their mouth, and if they move in the right direction with a gentle nudge, that is all there is to it. But if they refuse to move easily, they may get a kick in the flank as well as a jerk on the bit in their mouth. I think that is a perfect picture of how God moves us to where he wants us to be. We can go the easy way or the hard way, but in the end, "every knee shall bow." "God chastens those he loves."

REVELATIONS AND BREAKTHROUGHS can make us spiritually proud. Stay humble when you are elevated. It is said your true character is revealed with success. Always remember "it is God who gives great wealth, and he gives it without sorrow." Look to him and not the world for your success. When the world brings success and wealth, with it comes many sorrows.

DAY 160 June 9

"THE JUST SHALL live by faith." Living by faith is knowing and expecting that God will do what he says even when the circumstances look different. It is resting in the blessed assurance that he has his hand on you and is directing your path. It is believing mercy and grace shall follow you all the days of your life. It is trusting everything works together for good for you and that no weapon formed against you will prosper. It is believing you walk in divine health all the days of your life. Your joy is full. Yippee!

ANGER AND UNFORGIVENESS are never justified in the eyes of God. When you forgive someone, you are not doing them a favor. You are doing yourself a favor. Anger and unforgiveness are like poison in your body that will eat you from the inside out. There are probably hundreds of times every day in our lives that we can choose to be angry and offended by someone. Forgiveness is a choice! "Forgive that you may be forgiven."

Day 161   June 10

WE ARE THE ruler of our own life. Your life will be nothing more than you make it! It is up to you. It is no one else's fault what happens in your life. Take ownership of your life, your thoughts, your decisions, your emotions, your actions, your words. They all matter. Subdue the world that is within you. Take charge and believe you can and will make the changes necessary to become all you were meant to be. "Do all you know to do and then wait on God."

YOU CAN'T CHANGE the world, but you can make a difference in your own personal space. We all have influence within our own realm of life, and if we choose to set the example within those parameters, it can grow like a snowball. Never think your actions are irrelevant. "As iron sharpens iron, the countenance of a friend sharpens a friend." Your countenance matters!

Day 162   June 11

"I WILL CONTEND with those who contend with you, and I will save your children." What an amazing promise this is for both you and your children. Whenever someone does you wrong, if you look to God, he will fight your battle for you. The minute you get in there and try to use the arm of the flesh to win a battle, you eliminate God from the process. God will contend for those who contend with you. Get it? If you are in the right, God will fight your battles! And remember, he will also save your children. Wow!

RAGE IS EVERY coward's safest harbor. Rage serves to isolate. It prevents logical communication and drives a wedge between people. It is a copout in a very real sense. "The anger of men will never accomplish the purposes of God." Rage and anger will open the door to all sorts of evil workings. Ask God to give you strength sufficient for the day to operate in a godly, calm manner, no matter the situation.

Day 163   June 12

THE WAY WE feel will affect the way we act. Our mind is a battlefield. Ungodly influences, teaching, and indoctrination will destroy a country. A mentality becomes a stronghold. A stronghold once built in the minds will become a powerful destructive force in lives. There is a hostile system in the world that is against God, and it is appealing to the fallen man. Stay close to God and protect yourself from this stronghold. "Those who keep their mind on Christ will stay in perfect peace."

GOD IS NOT shown in your life by just your words, but the expression of the hands and body will also present God to the world. We can espouse the Word of God till we are blue in the face, but words can be destroyed by the work of the hands and the antics of the body. Be intentional about including your whole person as you witness to the world. "You will know them by their works."

DAY 164   June 13

THE HOLY SPIRIT will show up in your life just as Jesus showed up in the life of his twelve disciples. The Holy Spirit is the unseen spirit of God himself, just as Jesus was the visual spirit of God. The Holy Spirit will comfort you, give you hope and joy, and direct your steps. Tap into the Holy Spirit. "God draws close to those who draw close to him."

THERE IS A promise in the Bible that says, "God will restore the years the canker worms have eaten." If you have lost something in your life that meant a lot to you, claim this beautiful promise. God will restore everything that is ever taken, but many times we neglect to see the replacement, and instead we lament over the loss. Pay close attention to the new things that come into your life, and recognize and thank God for the new blessings. Those who give God praise for his goodness will always get more from God.

DAY 165   June 14

LIVE IN GRACE and walk in love. You do not have to win every argument or burn down the buildings of those who oppose you. Just love them. If you want to know where people are in their walk with the Lord, check how they treat those who disagree with them. This is the true test of the mature Christian. "You will know them by their works." The world rages, marches, throws stones, and burns flags because they do not know any better. We know better. Just love them. The Word does not say we have to like them, but it does say we have to love them.

SOMETIMES ANXIETY IS worse than the problem causing the anxiety. "God will give perfect peace to those who keep their mind on God." Anxiety is a common disorder in our culture, and yet God promises he will give his people perfect peace. Tap into this wonderful promise as you remind God of what he said because he tells us to "bring him in remembrance of his Word."

Day 166 June 15

WHATEVER IS TAKEN *for granted will eventually be taken away.* Treasure every precious thing you have in your life and never take those special things for granted. Things like your health, your youth, your parents, children, mates, friends, freedom, your country, and even stuff. There's nothing sadder than to lose something you took for granted, and as you look back, you finally realize what you had. Realize what you have before you lose it! "He who is faithful with what he has will become ruler over much."

DON'T TAKE YOUR difficulties out on other people just because you are going through hard times. When the going gets tough and you don't know what to do, keep doing what you do know to do. Keep moving forward, trusting that God will direct your steps. Get the scowl off your face and choose to enjoy life even in the midst of the trials. "The joy of the Lord is your strength."

DAY 167   June 16

WHEN YOU LOVE life, life will love you back. If you continually grumble and complain, you are fertilizing weeds. Your attitude about your life and the world around you will either be blessed or cursed by your thoughts and your words. Take care to "cast down wild imaginings that exalt themselves above God's Word." What you allow to stay in your thoughts will eventually come out your mouth, and what comes out your mouth will establish blessings or cursings. "The power of life and death is in the tongue."

SORROW AND REGRET is not full repentance. Hopefully it will turn to repentance, but it is not enough on its own. Repentance means to turn from what you have done. To stop doing it! Just being sorry is not enough. Repentance is not only a condition of the mind; it requires a physical action. It is not accurate to limit repentance to the mind. Repentance involves the heart and not just the emotions. "Sin no more. Repent and turn from your wicked ways."

Day 168 June 17

THE JOURNEY OF life is meant to be a dream quest that your maker has given you to fulfill his purpose for you. "God has a good plan for your life, a plan to prosper you and not to harm you." We are not meant to just bumble through life and never know our purpose. Give studious attention to your dreams because within those dreams will lie the purpose God has for you. Set your hand to what you have found and do your part to move towards those dreams with sure steps, even if they are baby steps, and little by little, you will find yourself living your dream.

"GOD WILL PERFECT that which concerns you." God is working on your behalf, and your part is to keep your hands moving and confess positive things. Find promises in the Bible and confess them out loud over your family, your home, your body, your business, your finances... God will bring to pass those things that you say often enough. Be sure what you are saying is what you want because that is what you will get.

Day 169   June 18

CHAOS DEFINED IS complete confusion and disorder. Chaos can enter our life in a moment's time, or it can slowly seep into our life, but it still brings feelings of hopelessness, confusion, and helplessness. But God says, "He will bring order from chaos." Sometimes your life can feel like chaos is surrounding you as random events seem to attack you. Tackle these things one at a time and remind God to help you bring order out of the mess. Keep moving as you complete one task at a time. This will pass.

GOD GIVES SPECIAL, unique gifts to everyone. And your gifts will pass down to your children and ancestors and, many times, will increase in volume and strength. When we "raise up our children, in my way they should go." God will often give our children a double anointing of what he gave us. Live your life well, knowing your life will be passed down to your children. "Blessings and cursings come down, even to the tenth generation."

Day 170   June 19

I PRAY A special blessing on all the men who read this, and I pray God will give you special insight into the needs of your children. Have a wonderful Father's Day.

SPEAKING INTO THE *heart of a boy has the power to save the life of a man.* I took this phrase from a book friend of mine wrote, and it is so powerful! Let that sink in on this Father's Day. I speak to the fathers out there who have perhaps frivolously or even haphazardly fathered your children. Be assured your actions have a direct impact on your offspring. It is never too late to ask God to help you be one of those who speak into the heart of a boy and change his life. "Like arrows in the hands of a warrior are your children. Blessed is the man whose quiver is full of them." Thankfully it is not how you start that is counted but rather how you finish. Finish well. Have a blessed day with your family. Happy Father's Day.

DAY 171   June 20

SOMETIMES IT IS so hard to understand why God makes us wait for something. We may or may not realize why we had to wait, but God has a timing in place that is in your best interest. Be at peace about that and just wait. "Those who wait on the Lord shall renew their strength, they shall rise up with wings like eagles, they shall run and not grow weary, they shall walk and not faint."

MAKE A CONSCIOUS effort to believe the best in people. When you see someone who is being offensive, make a real effort to try to understand them rather than to strike out and be angry. We never know what's really in the heart of others when they are acting rude, disrespectful, or even downright hateful. "Be kind and compassionate to one another, forgiving each other, just as Christ forgave you."

"WHEN GOD MAKES rich, he does not bring any sorrow with it." Money and stuff can actually make people miserable unless it is given from God. The rich man is constantly fretting over losing his riches. People like them because they have money, so they don't trust people because they think everybody wants something from them. There are all kinds of reasons that being wealthy makes men unhappy. But on the other hand, if God brings the riches, it brings great joy. Thank you, Lord.

WE CAN GAIN victories over the things that are wrong in our life, whether it be physical, financial, spiritual, or a relationship, but victory will only come in "the presence of God." Do not give up on God. Stay in his presence. Pray, go to church, listen to Christian music, do Bible study, hang around with good, godly, like-minded people, and believe that a miracle is going to happen at any moment. "Do not depart from his presence or his Word and you will prosper in all that you do."

Day 173   June 22

FAILURE IS SIMPLY *the opportunity to begin again and, this time, more intelligently.* Those who fail and choose to try again have an equivalent to a master's degree! It should never be considered a loss, and if you fail a second or even a third time, you get your PhD! Never give up! Learn from your mistakes and include God as you begin again. If you keep swinging the bat, sooner or later you WILL hit a home run! "The wise man learns by watching, while the fool has to have a rod taken to his back." Watch and learn.

"GET BACK TO basics." Sometimes we get so totally engrossed in the flamboyancy of life that we miss the obvious. The basics are all the little keys to success. The small things don't usually carry the fanfare, as do the extravagant deeds, so they are often left unchecked and forgotten. These little things are the difference between success and failure. "He who is faithful in the little things will become ruler over much."

Day 174   June 23

GOD DOES NOT ask us to be perfect, but he does ask us to give him our best. "Never compare yourself one to the other," but be the absolute best you can be. Not the best of someone else, but only your best. We all have our gifts and things we are good at, and others have their gifts. If you compare yourself to others, you will either become pompous or insecure. Just do the best you can and then thank God for the abilities he has given you.

BUILD A STRONG wall of faith around your life and the life of your family. Walls are the outward manifestation of your strength and your faith. Walls are necessary. Not because you do not love others but because you love your family and those behind those walls. It is pure foolishness to think all people can be trusted. "Be wise as a serpent and gentle as a dove."

Day 175   June 24

PSALM 11:3–4 SAYS, "When the foundations are being destroyed, what can the righteous do? The Lord is in his holy temple, and he is on his heavenly throne." What we as believers can do is trust God and know he's not a magical, mythical character but rather an omnipotent God who is in control of our flimsy little earth. Do not put your trust in man. The arm of the flesh can never supersede what God has ordained! Those who think that the wise, educated men will figure this out are putting their trust in the wind. "God uses the foolishness of men to confound the wise." "The beginning of wisdom is the fear of the Lord."

IF YOU DO not exercise judgments on yourself, you will be swallowed up by consequential judgments as you reap the consequences of your lack of control on your own life. If you take charge of your own errors, you can escape much of the sorrow that accompanies the average life. Be willing to face your sins and errors and "confess your sins one to the other that you might be saved." Do yourself a favor and find a trusted friend and spill the beans.

Day 176   June 25

"FEAR NOT" IS in the Bible 365 times. One for every day of the year. There are three kinds of fear. The first is the fear of the Lord, and this is a good fear, as it represents respect and honor. Second is a fear of timidity or insecurity. Remember "perfect love casts out all fear" when you know who you are in the Lord. The third fear is the one that encompasses the over two thousand fears known to mankind. It is debilitating, and it is a lack of understanding of who and what God can do for you. Press into God and get to know him. "Call unto God, and he will deliver you from all of your fears." I know this works because I did it.

GOD SEES THE other side of our failure. He knows the beginning from the end, and incredibly, his plan is to work those failures towards good. Never beat yourself up because you failed. Instead look for the treasure hidden within the failure. "I will show you the hidden treasures in dark secret places."

DAY 177   June 26

YOUR WORDS, WHEN they agree with God, are the nails you will build or construct your life with. There is not a more powerful weapon against the enemy than using the Word of God with your lips. "Speak to the mountains in your life and tell them to be removed, and if you believe in your heart and do not doubt, they will go." Keep in mind that God's Word is true no matter what you believe, but it is not activated in your life until you believe. There comes a time that you stop talking to God about the mountains in your life and start talking to the mountains and tell them to "be removed, in Jesus's name."

WE ALL HAVE a soft, sweet side. This is a God-given gift to every human. It is our place to protect and preserve that soft sweetness within. Do not harden your heart or allow others to mess around with this sweetness that God has given you. This sweetness lives in your heart. Cultivate and feed it, and it will grow. "Above all else, protect the heart because from within the heart flows the issues of life."

Day 178 June 27

WE CANNOT ALWAYS understand why God heals some people and does not heal others, but that should never discourage your faith in what God can do for you. "Don't compare yourself one to the other." God has ordained a plan for each life, and if we stay in the parameters he has set, the plan will come to fruition. Sometimes it includes trials we don't like, but if we keep our faith and trust God through it all, everything that happens to us will work towards good. It's all part of the plan.

GOD WILL OFTEN allow evil to reign for a time in order to accomplish his plan. Do not fret over evil but pray and ask God to work it towards good. God will often allow the enemy to test you. Stand strong through these trials and you will emerge a different, stronger person. God sifts us. "God may allow you to be stricken down but not destroyed. He will uphold you with his right hand." Trust him.

DAY 179   June 28

DO NOT ALLOW your insecurities or insufficiencies to stop your progress in life. Mistakes happen in life, and they can propel you to success if you learn from them. Do not let your past failures convince you that you cannot do it. You are more qualified because of your failures. There are way more successes the second time around. "Forget those things that are behind and reach towards those things that are ahead."

GOD TELLS US to "pray for those who have mistreated us." And to pray a blessing upon them. When we are really mad at someone, this is hard to do because we don't want our enemies blessed. But remember this: when you pray a blessing on someone, the very first thing God is going to do is to bless them with truth. You're not praying for a new car or new house for them. It is not that kind of blessing. It is God's blessing of enlightenment and truths that will bring them to repentance.

Day 180 June 29

MAKE ROOM IN life for people to make mistakes. We all make them. It seems everyone today is so quick to judge and get angry rather than to show the mercy God shows to us. Remember that "when you show mercy, mercy will be shown to you." Life is full of mistakes, and all of us add to those mistakes daily. Forgive yourself and forgive others. Unforgiveness will always end tragically. I sincerely believe unforgiveness is one of the main causes for failure in life. FORGIVE!

GOD DOESN'T TELL us to not be angry, but he does say, "Be angry, but do not sin," and then he says, "Do not let the sun go down on your wrath," so he gives us a period of time to work through our anger. He understands that you get angry, but he does not allow us to hang on to that anger. Get your sulking out before the day ends, and "pray for those who have mistreated you, and in so doing, you bring coals of fire [shame] down on their head."

Day 181   June 30

BE CONFIDENT WHEN you pray that God hears you and he will honor your prayers if it is prayed with a sincere heart and with faith. Your prayers are powerful. There are those who do not have any faith in their own prayers. They think that someone else needs to pray for them, and agreement is powerful, but your singular prayer is perfect. It does not have to be eloquent. It is just you talking to your Father in heaven. "The effectual fervent prayer of a righteous man avails much."

I DON'T THINK anyone ever goes through life without having seasons of weakness and vulnerability. We all have experienced this at least once, and many times it comes on and off throughout our life. This does not mean God is not with you. God says, "I will never leave you nor forsake you." These seasons come from your own insecurities. Walk through them as you press into God. Stir yourself up by reading the Bible, singing praises, listening to Christian music, and giving thanks out loud. This works every time.

July

THE STRENGTH OF your faith will determine your destiny. While we are all given the same measure of faith at birth, we do not all end up with the same amount. Like a muscle, faith is increased with use and by reading the Word. "Faith comes by hearing the Word of God." Strong, mature faith will change a life. Baby faith is sweet for babies, but if you want to move mountains and battle the trials of life, you are going to need a buff faith. "Study to make yourself approved."

STRIVING FOR EXCELLENCE is not even in the same category as perfectionism. Excellence is something we should all strive for, but perfectionism is dangerous and generally nothing more than nitpicking. Perfectionism is never satisfied, it annoys everyone around you, and it creates a lack of appreciation for anything because nothing is ever perfect except God. "Be careful when you think you stand, lest you fall."

DAY 183   July 2

"DO NOT LET the sun go down on your wrath." How many times have you gone to bed angry at someone? There are times in our life that it is so difficult to forgive someone, but every time we choose to step out of God's perimeter, we are stepping out from under his protective umbrella. We cannot do things the way we want and expect God's Word to work in our lives! If he says something, doggone it, we have got to do it that way! You are only hurting yourself more if you don't forgive. Forgiveness of someone does not mean you approve of them or their actions. It does not mean you accept them back into your life. God knows how hard it is for us to forgive, but once you say it out loud, he will help you. And to walk through this life without God's forgiveness is horrifying to me.

OUR GOD CAN and will take the crooked places in your life and make them straight, and incredibly, those crooked places will become the highlights of your life because "it is in your weakness that God is made strong." Give your life and all your tweaks over to God. "He is faithful to finish the work he has started in you."

Day 184   July 3

SIN IS LIKE quicksand. It will always take you to an unexpected extreme. When you think you can dabble in sin, you are playing Russian roulette, and I guarantee you that your famine is coming! You will not escape famine! "Be careful when you think you stand, lest you fall." God's arms are open and waiting, and he can and will work those killer sins towards good. "Draw close to him, and he will draw close to you."

DO NOT EXPECT man to praise you or even thank you for the good you do, but God always sees and rewards the good a person does. "Whatever good thing one man does for another, God will do for him." Your expectations of people will bring disappointment every time. When you give, just give, and don't expect anything back. "What you do in secret, God will reward openly." The Word says, "Don't even let your right hand know what your left hand is doing." Just do it! No expectations!

Day 185   July 4

PSALM 33:12 SAYS, "Blessed is the nation whose God is the Lord, the people whom he has chosen as his heritage!" America has always rested under that blessed assurance. I feel so troubled as I watch our country pulling away from God, seeing men and women take over who think they don't need God and are blatantly thumbing their nose at many of the divine parameters he has set for mankind. We can already see the results as we look at the division and unrest in our country. Pray fervently for God to forgive us and establish a government that truly believes we are "one nation under God."

"THERE IS NO condemnation to those who are in Christ Jesus," but we are not given this freedom as an opportunity for our flesh to run rampant. I often see Christians who think they can live like hell because they are covered by this wonderful scripture that promises us that Jesus took all of our sins. Be not deceived because, "as you sow, you are going to reap." Even if you are born again and covered with the blood of Jesus, you are still subject to the ramifications of sin. In fact, when you know better and you continue to sin anyway, "you are trampling underfoot the blood of Jesus." A very scary place to find yourself.

DAY 186 July 5

JUST BECAUSE YOU still remember what someone did to you, does not mean you have not forgiven them. We are ordered by God to forgive others. When someone has harmed you, it may take years for the wound to heal, and even when it does, there is usually a scar left behind. Do not trouble yourself with the remembrance of what someone did. But say out loud that you forgive them, and pray for them. God says to "pray for those who have mistreated you, and in so doing, you bring the coals of fiery shame down on their head."

IF YOU STAY close to God, you will always stay on course. The world is full of all sorts of distractions, and it is easy to wander off the track, but if you are pressing into God, he will always keep you on his holy highway where no evil thing may travel, where your footing is sure and you can always see beautiful scenery, even as the world rages around you.

DAY 187   July 6

JESUS DOES NOT love you more when you do good, nor does he love you less when you do bad. He loves all his children unconditionally. He is certainly pleased with good behavior and certainly grieved with bad behavior, but he still loves everyone equally. Do not wait to come to God because you feel unworthy. The simplicity of your choice to ask God into your heart will start the work that he is faithful to finish.

BE CAREFUL THAT demands on your time are not stolen by an agent of evil who would like to distract you from what God has planned for your life. God tells us to "be as wise as the serpent and gentle as a lamb." Sometimes we forget to be wise as a serpent and trust too easily. Be sure when you are directed to a time-consuming project that it is something God has planned for you. I love the scripture that says, "Out of the mouth of two or three witnesses, a truth becomes established." Listen for truths to be confirmed through godly trusted people.

DAY 188 July 7

FAITH IN GOD can move mountains, but we have to participate. Whether you believe in faith or not does not change what faith can do, but it will change what faith can do for you. Your participation in the promises of God is almost always needed. Once in a while, God will do a miracle without your participation. But more times than not, you have to do your part to make God's miracles work in your life. "Faith without works is dead."

DON'T SAY NEGATIVE things about yourself or your loved ones. Words can break up family, they can hurt, destroy a job, discourage, injure a child for life, or they can make a friend, heal, convince, and encourage. Jesus said they can even move a mountain! Words are powerful! Use your words to build up rather than to tear down. "Pleasant words are like a honeycomb, sweet to the soul and health to the bones."

DAY 189   July 8

"BE NOT DECEIVED, bad company corrupts good behavior." While we are called to love everyone, we should not assume we can continually mingle with ungodly people and believe we will not be affected. "Like attracts like," and an assessment of your friends will pretty much tell you what you are like. Choose close friends that enhance your life, even as you are kind to everyone.

IT IS SAID that *Luck is where preparation meets opportunity*. I often hear people say they are unlucky. You will never find someone who is lucky if they claim they are not. Luck is nothing more than expectation, but it is also doing your part to make things happen. God's favor on your life can make you appear to be lucky because, as he directs your path and you do your part, success will prevail. "The Lord bestows favor and honor. No good thing does he withhold from those who walk uprightly."

Day 190   July 9

IN THE DARK *and meanest things, something, something always sings.* Do you walk with a spirit of contentment or a spirit of complaint? Because your life will reflect your choice. We have a choice to see the glass half full, or we can choose to see it half empty. There is always an opportunity to complain about things because nothing is perfect, but if you can choose to see the beauty even in the mud and scum of things, life will be full of joy and excitement. "This is the day the Lord has made. I will rejoice and be glad in it."

BE A TEAM player in your life. Do not choose to do life alone. Together we are strong. "It is not good for man to be alone." Accept those people who are strategically placed in your life. Learn from them even as they learn from you. Do not compete with your own team! I am convinced that a need to outdo others will weaken you as well as others. "Two are better than one because they have a good reward for their work."

DAY 191   July 10

JUST BECAUSE YOU cannot see a wound on people does not mean they are not wounded, and healing only happens when you become honest. If you continue to hide your issues, God will not heal you. It is not only healthy, but it is a wise choice to admit to a hidden wound. If you hide your wounds, they will never get healed! "Confess your sins one to the other that you might be healed."

DEMANDS ON YOUR time can be distracting from the really important things God has for you. Just because the world demands things from you, you do not have to comply. We always need to be loving and kind, but we cannot be available to and for everyone. Just as a fruit tree needs to be thinned or the fruit will be small and not as sweet, our time is the same. If we try to accommodate everyone, we will not be able to provide much to anyone. Be selective and use your time wisely. "Acknowledge God, and he will direct your steps."

DAY 192   July 11

GOD PROMISES THAT "he will restore your health and fix your brokenness." That is an amazing promise, and even though our flesh is susceptible to the things of the earth, God knows how to repair everything. God made our bodies in such a way that they are capable of completely healing themselves. Do your part by caring for your flesh. Eat right, exercise, get plenty of sleep, and drink lots of water as you acknowledge God in all your ways. And God will do the rest, he promises!

YOU NEVER KNOW how God will choose to answer a prayer, and don't expect him to do it the same way he did it last time or how you think it should be done. The only time you will find God in a box is if he comes in there to visit you. "His ways are higher than your ways," and your puny mind will never totally understand the mysteries of God. Pray and then relax in the knowledge God knows how to handle your problem. "Only believe."

DAY 193   July 12

GOALS, OBJECTIVES, AND a path that includes God. Add perseverance and hard work to that, and voila! Success! This statement almost goes without any explanation. Set your goals, which include your loved ones as well as the desires of your heart. "He works in you to will and to do his good pleasure." Ask for God's direction. "God will direct your path" and keep your hands moving. "God will bless the work of your hands," and then stay the course. "Grow not weary of well doing because, in due season, you still have your reward." It's all laid out for us. All we have to do is do it!

"THE FEAR OF man brings a snare, but whoever trusts in the Lord shall be safe." In other words, if your fear and respect lies in men, you are setting a trap for yourself because men can never do for you what God can do. If you put your hopes and expectations on men, you will always be disappointed, but "those who put their trust in God will never be disappointed."

DAY 194   July 13

REMEMBER THE "HELP me" prayer is the most powerful prayer you will ever pray. You do not have to tell God how to answer your prayer. He knows your needs, and the simplicity of "help me" invites God in! Eloquent prayers are not necessary. I have heard people say, "I don't know how to pray." Hello! HELP ME! A kindergartner can pray this powerful prayer. Try it.

YOUR ETERNAL PERSPECTIVE should affect your earthly priorities. An eternal perspective will make your life better. Every single thing you go through is purifying you. It is predestined and part of the journey God knows must happen to sanctify you for himself. Just as the heat and pressure of an iron removes wrinkles from our clothes, heat and pressure also irons out the wrinkles in our life and character. "Count it all joy when you go through the fiery trials because it is perfecting you."

DAY 195   July 14

WHEN YOU HAVE been wronged by someone, look to God and ask him to vindicate you. Ask him to do something that will prove your innocence. Do not try to take things into your own hands, or things might get worse. Take your grievance to God and tattle to your heavenly Father, just as you would to your earthly father. We serve a just God, and if you put your faith in him, he will see that justice is done. Remember to "pray for those who mistreat you, as this will bring coals of fiery shame upon their heads, and the Lord will reward you."

TELL GOD WHAT you need of him. Jesus needs to know what you need him to do for you. He is a gentleman and will not interfere until you ask. "You have not because you ask not." Stop and consider your own needs and earnestly ask God what you would like for him to do for you. And then expect to receive. "As you believe, it is done unto you." "Jesus have mercy on me."

DAY 196   July 15

FROM A DICTIONARY perspective, the opposite of belief is unbelief, but according to the Bible, the opposite of belief is FEAR! Belief is another word for faith, and fear and faith cannot operate at the same time, and faith is the only thing that pleases God. The beginning of fear is the end of faith. And the beginning of true faith is the end of fear! Did you get all that?

SOMETIMES FAILURE IS simply God protecting you from getting good at something you're not supposed to be doing. Failure is never a failure if you've learned something from it. When you trust God, failure is not even part of the equation but rather a part of the destiny that he has planned for you. Never kick the tires when you get a flat tire. You never know what you were being protected from. "Trust God with all your heart and lean not on your own understanding."

DAY 197   July 16

IT IS ONE thing to be a servant to others and be there for them when the sun is shining and all is well, but it is another whole level of servant when you help others in your own times of troubles or need. When things have gone amok in your life, sometimes the best thing you can do is reach out to others. The Word says that as we "pray one for the other, we are healed ourselves." God blesses those the most who choose to bless others. He will enrich in every way those who are generous with not only their stuff but with their time.

DOUBT WILL HINDER your prayers! Remember that "as you believe, it is done unto you." When you have prayed, "believe you have received." When you don't believe, it doesn't change God's Word, but it will change how it affects your life. Make a choice to believe God's Word even if it doesn't make sense to you. You do not have to understand God's Word to have it work in your life. God makes it so easy! He says, "Only believe."

Day 198   July 17

THE CARNAL MIND and its way of thinking are an enemy to God. Men talk about science, and many trust science more than they trust God. Bring your thoughts into captivity and cast down anything that exalts itself above God. "Thank God for science, but always remember God supersedes science. And remember it is God who gives the creative ideas scientists come up with. Give God the glory, not man! "All good things come from above."

DO NOT ALLOW your insecurities or insufficiencies to stop your progress in life. Mistakes happen in life, and they can propel you to success if you learn from them. Do not let your past failures convince you that you cannot do it. You are more qualified because of your failures. There are way more successes the second time around. "Forget those things that are behind and reach towards those things that are ahead."

DAY 199   July 18

YOU CANNOT GET where you want to go if you do not know your starting place or what your current reality is. Magical thinking is wonderful, but it isn't always realistic. Never stop dreaming or thinking magically, but always analyze the reality of your dreams and visions, and be sure to include God, keeping in mind that "as you delight yourself in the Lord, he will give you the desires of your heart." Sometimes your magical thinking may be impossible for you, but always remember "nothing is impossible for God."

NEVER LET YOUR experience determine your faith. Make a choice to believe God's Word, no matter what you may see with your eyes. Always choose to believe in the power of the unseen world because "all things are possible to him who believes." Ask God to help your unbelief. We all struggle with unbelief, but the victorious will choose to push through as they choose to believe, no matter what. "In due season you will have your reward."

Day 200   July 19

MANY TIMES, PEOPLE reject God because they are blinded by the deception of sin. They actually do not realize the profundity of the consequences of sin. Horrendous crimes are often committed when someone is out of their right mind, but repentance is still necessary. Sin never goes without punishment, even when it is done out of ignorance. Sinning in ignorance is still sin. But the good news is that no sin is too big for God to forgive. Place your sin under the blood of Jesus by asking for forgiveness, and you have a clean slate. "When you have asked God for forgiveness of your sins, he does not even remember them anymore."

NEVER LOSE SIGHT of the fact that your decisions and what you do will produce consequences, both good and bad. It is vital to your spiritual growth and well-being that you consider the outcome of choices and actions. A single bad choice can set your life on a course of destruction. "Acknowledge God in all your ways, and he will make your path straight."

Day 201

July 20

THE FORCE OF God's favor on your life is irresistible, and if you couple that favor with the spirit of endurance and perseverance, you become unstoppable where men are concerned. The value of God's gift of favor on your life is only second to your salvation. When you seek to serve God, you choose to do what is right, and you delight yourself in God, his favor will fall on you. This will cause men to be drawn to you, giving you an advantage in life. "Seek first the kingdom of God and his righteousness, and all of these things shall be added unto you."

"THOSE WHO OPPOSE the Lord will be shattered." I find it shocking to see how many people are actually rebelling boldly against God. In the end, they will be obliterated. There is no way any puny human can oppose God and get away with it. He is patient and gives everybody a chance to repent. But in the end, he always wins! "One day every knee shall bow."

Day 202   July 21

"SUCH AS YOU perceive, you become." And "wherever you look, you will go." Keep good, positive, productive thoughts in your head and keep your focus on exactly where you want to go. Because your body will follow where your eyes stray. Make an intentional effort to see the good in things and do not allow your head to be turned by negative, nasty, ungodly things. "Your flesh is weak, but your spirit is strong." Do not allow your physical body to control your destiny. Let your spirit take charge.

THE PURPOSES OF God are not based on your ability but rather how he is able to work through you. God will often call the unqualified simply because they are willing vessels, and ultimately, he will always qualify the called. Be willing to do what God wants from you. Be willing to tell God, "Here I am Lord. Send me." When you choose to do God's perfect will for you, you will find pure joy.

Day 203   July 22

DID YOU KNOW your faith can heal you? If we as believers could really, really believe God's Word, we would never need a doctor. God made our bodies in such a way that they are capable of completely healing themselves. Sin and unbelief have almost completely hindered that ability. I pray for myself and every believer reading this that we would be able to operate in this beautiful promise of God to the extent that we can believe and receive God's promises in every area of our life, including physical healing. "Only believe."

SOME OF THE best lessons are learned from the errors of the past. When we have made a mistake, it is useless to lament over it if we learned a lesson from it. Mistakes always carry with them a learning curve. "A wise man learns by watching the mistakes of others and himself, while a fool has to have a rod taken to his back." If we don't learn from our mistakes, we are destined to repeat them.

Day 204   July 23

OFTEN, DIFFICULT ROADS lead to beautiful destinations. Though it may seem you are bound and cannot see the light at the end of the tunnel, keep moving forward, even if it is baby steps. Walk out the journey and expect to see the good life God has planned for you. "God has a good plan for your life, a plan to prosper you and not to harm you, plans to give you hope and a future." Only believe because as you believe, so it is.

KEEP SERVING GOD, even though you're sad. When we serve God and others, it will lift up our soul. Do not choose to sit and wallow in your sadness. Remember that our book of instructions says, "Praise for the spirit of heaviness." Heaviness is oppression, depression, grief, and even apathy. It is perfectly natural to stop once in a while and grieve and even cry. But don't sit there too long and wallow in your sorrow. Praise and thank God for everything in your life. Sorrows come and go, but "God is the same yesterday, today, and tomorrow."

DAY 205   July 24

IN LUKE 1:9, God tells us that if you are persistent and you keep asking, you will get what you ask for. I'm always amazed at people who say, "I never ask for anything for myself." That sounds real sweet and pious, but God says, "You have not because you ask not." It is completely acceptable and even required that you pray for yourself as well as for others. And then after you have asked, "believe you have received" and be persistent in reminding God of your request.

LOVE AND REVERENCE are the keys to receiving God's favor and extreme blessings. Reverence is the direct result of revelation. In other words, when you really understand the magnificence of God, this brings about reverence and causes you to adore God. The word adore is a combination of love, respect, and honor. When you truly adore God and you "delight yourself in him, he will give you the desires of your heart."

DAY 206   July 25

NEVER CHOOSE TO add to the burdens of others for your own personal gain. Be a blessing rather than a burden. And be that one person who steps forward to persevere for those who are carrying a burden. Selfishness heaps burdens on others, and it will always lead to a breakdown in relationships. "Consider others more important than yourself." I believe that is the most important scripture for having a beautiful successful marriage and sincere long friendships.

WHAT PEOPLE BELIEVE prevails over the truth, and this should not be. Truth should always prevail over your opinion or the opinion of others. God says, "The wisdom of man is foolishness to God." When you choose to set your opinion ahead of what God says, you are truly making a fool of yourself and separating yourself from God and his wisdom. Truth is truth, and opinions can never hold a candle to what is true. Always stay open to receive truth.

DAY 207   July 26

IN YOUTH, WE learn. In age, we understand. The Bible says, "Gray hair is a sign of wisdom." It is wise to listen to elders who have been around the Horn. There's nothing more obnoxious than a young person who thinks they know it all and are not teachable. Always be willing to glean from those who have learned valuable lessons through their own experiences. "Listen to the instructions and be wise. Do not ignore it."

HOW BLESSED IS the man who does not walk in the counsel of the wicked, nor stand in the path of sinners, nor sit in the seat of scoffers! What delight comes to the one who follows God's ways! I believe we are to be kind to sinners, but we should stay in the presence of those who love the Lord. God says, "Be not deceived, bad company corrupts good behavior." Be nice to everyone, but steer clear of those who might corrupt your behavior.

CAST DOWN ALL thoughts that come into your mind that are averse to anything that exalts itself against the Word of God. Negative thoughts are not a sin unless you entertain those thoughts. It is natural to have bad thoughts come into your carnal mind, but if you allow these thoughts to germinate, they will eventually become a reality in your life, your mind will become hardened, and this will separate you from God. "Keep your mind on the things above rather than the things below."

THOSE WHO PUNCH God forget about the consequences of reaping and sowing. When it seems the wicked prosper without consequences, it is just God allowing them to fill their cup of iniquity before his judgment falls on them. Rest assured that justice will be done! The law of reaping and sowing will always fulfill itself. "There is a time and season for everything under the sun."

DAY 209 July 28

PROVERBS 17:4 SAYS, "Evil people listen to evil ideas, and liars listen to lies." There are times a scripture is so profound that it doesn't even need any words put with it. I believe this is one of those scriptures. There is so much evil and too many lies going around. Let's make a conscious choice to not be part of that. And by the way, if you are watching any of the major news channels, you are listening to lies. What does that make you?

GOD WILL "ENLARGE the path under your feet and keep you from slipping." When you first begin your walk with the Lord, the path seems narrow, but as you continue this journey, the path will actually seem wider and easier to follow. This is your unique path that God has chosen for you, and I cannot even imagine taking any other route. This path is filled with joy, peace, blessings, and pure comfort. It will protect you from all the evil things rampant in the world today. Stay on your path, and you will be led to exactly where you are supposed to be.

DAY 210   July 29

LIFE ITSELF WILL challenge your faith. There is always something going on in life that will cause you to question God and his promises. Make an intentional decision that no matter what you see with your eyes, things will get better! The size of your faith does not matter. It is what you put your faith in that matters. "Faith the size of a mustard seed can move a mountain." Natural limitations do not affect God. "With man some things are impossible, but with God all things are possible."

PERSEVERANCE IS THE most important ingredient to success. You can have every talent and every opportunity in the world, but if you cannot or will not persevere, you will never be successful. I have watched people over the years who had amazing potential who never went anywhere because of a lack of perseverance. Make a choice to stay put, and God will honor your faithfulness. "When you're faithful with a little, you will get a lot."

DAY 211   July 30

A BREAKTHROUGH WILL often seem like it happened suddenly, when in fact it is usually the culmination of perseverance. A continuous axing to a tree trunk will eventually take the tree down, and even though the tree falls suddenly, in actuality, it has been an arduous task of a continuation of hacking on the tree. If you want a breakthrough, you can't give up. This includes every single facet of life. You must continue pressing through. "In due season you shall have your reward."

THE ALLOWANCE OF God will never let you suffer more than you can handle. Oftentimes God allows suffering in our lives for a purpose. Just as you may need to go over a bumpy road to get to a certain destination, so goes our life. There are things that must happen in order to get us to the place God is taking us. "Count it all joy when you go to the fiery trials because it is perfecting you." Keep moving and praise God every inch of the way.

WHEREVER GOD IS removed, chaos will fill the void! When God was removed from schools, the vacuum that was left has been filled with evil. It is not guns, religion, or politics that are doing it, folks. It is the removal of God! When evil prevails, those who are used by the enemy will find the means to destroy. If we would just wake up in America and take a look at what has happened since God was taken out of our schools and from everything public, I think we could find a good part of our problem. Without God, "everything is meaningless. It's chasing after the wind."

August

LOVE THAT HAS no choice is not love. We cannot force people to love us, and this goes for our children. Sometimes, for whatever reason, there will be those in our life who refuse to love us. I often see grown children who choose to separate themselves from their parents. While this is hurtful to the parent, we cannot change their decision. Do the best you can to accept this choice as you continue to pray and do your part to love them. "The fervent prayer of a righteous man avails much."

DOUBT WILL HINDER your prayers! Remember that "as you believe, it is done unto you." When you have prayed, "believe you have received." When you don't believe, it doesn't change God's Word, but it will change how it affects your life. Make a choice to believe God's Word even if it doesn't make sense to you. You do not have to understand God's Word to have it work in your life. God makes it so easy! He says, "Only believe."

DAY 214   August 2

STUDIES SHOW THAT we tend to think of ourselves based on what the most important person in our life thinks of us. This can be such a troublesome situation because the favor of men cannot be trusted. It is fickle, competitive, and many times unfair. This is where the love of God can change the character of an individual. When you know how much God loves you and you are committed to pleasing him rather than man, you will find you think you are pretty doggone special. Open your heart to the love of God. No one will ever love you like he does.

THE SELF-CONTROL spoken of in the Bible is not the self-control you already have, but rather it is going above and beyond our natural giftings. Some things you find difficult are easy for some, just as some of your natural gifts are difficult for others. There are some things that come easy. Work on the Bible kind of self-control, which works hard at those things that take real self-control. "Like a city whose walls are broken through is a person who lacks self-control."

DAY 215   August 3

IT IS SAID that when you have had a true encounter with Jesus, you walk with a limp rather than with a strut. The revelation of who Jesus is will cause a person to walk humbly. People often say Jesus is a crutch for the weak, but the truth is he is the strength for all of us. Those who think they are strong without Jesus are deceived, and the time will come when they realize the arm of the flesh cannot fight the battles of life for us. We all need Jesus. "I am weak, but Jesus is strong."

GOD SAYS, "IF you seek me, you will find me." It is up to us to find God. And when you find him, you will also find your destiny. They go hand in hand. It is up to us to seek God. He is there waiting for you, but he will never push himself on you. As you seek him, you will be directed towards that which will fulfill your soul. "God has a plan for you, and it is a good plan, a plan to prosper you and not to harm you."

DAY 216   August 4

THE BELIEVER GAINS the inward presence of God himself, as he actually dwells in those who give their life over to him. Just imagine this great news! No matter what you may think of yourself, God actually dwells in you. Wow, that's pretty impressive, and I believe that if we could really grasp that, we would be able to move mountains. It is only our own doubt and unbelief that restrains us. "I can do all things through Christ who strengthens me."

CHASING AFTER WORLDLY contentment is like a hamster running on a wheel for hours and getting absolutely nowhere. The world has nothing to offer that is eternal or consistent, it is never fulfilling, and it always takes more and more to satisfy. The flesh will crave more and more while it searches for that satisfied feeling that only God can give. It's not the new and improved flashy toy that makes you happy but the same old Jesus, who has always been there and always will be there. "God is the same yesterday, today, and tomorrow."

Day 217   August 5

CIRCUMSTANCES SHOULD NEVER define your hope because life is a bumpy road. There will always be ups and downs, but none of this affects God's promises. His Word never changes. It is "the same yesterday, today, and tomorrow." God never promised that life would be easy, but he did promise he would always be with us and walk through the troubled times with us. Put your confidence in God. "Those who put their trust in God will never be disappointed."

MANY TIMES, A deception will come in the form of danger. If you are in line with God and you are doing what is right, you are never in danger! That is a lie of the enemy. The enemy uses fear more times than anything else to deceive you into believing you cannot do what God has called you to do. We are only in danger when we violate our own core values. We instinctively know what God expects from us. Stay under God's protective covering, and danger cannot touch you. It is a deception.

YOU WILL NEVER have to go through anything alone if you have latched on to God. He will travel every journey with you. He will guide and comfort you every step of the way. Love, joy, peace, patience, and kindness will grace your life as you walk on the holy highway that is narrow and straight yet filled with amazing, treasured sights and sounds. A highway that no evil thing may come upon. A highway that leads to your promised land.

WE CAN SPEND our days focusing on all the what-ifs, or we can focus on what magnificent thing could come out of this mess. Always face fear with faith and hope. Fear is *False Evidence Appearing Real*. There are horrible things that will happen in life, but we will always be able to overcome, as "God gives us the strength sufficient for the day." Mishaps will always work towards good when we serve God and stand in faith. If your decisions are based on fear, you have been deceived. "Keep your eyes on the things above and not on the things below."

Day 219   August 7

PICK YOUR BATTLES! We can spend our life bickering and arguing over small things, or we can choose to defend and be selective in the things that really matter. Most disagreements can be thwarted by simply keeping your mouth shut! "There is no contention if there is no contender." It is foolish and a waste of time to spend your days arguing with someone over irrelevant trivia or something you have no control over. "We are called to a life of peace." Do your part by being tolerant and respectful of opposing opinions.

WHEN REFLECTING BACK on your life, rejoice in your victories instead of lamenting over your failures. Your mistakes have helped to shape your character and your ability to overcome has developed strength. Encourage yourself by remembering your own victories. Life is an outrageous journey filled with tons of beautiful, wonderful, exciting moments interspersed with many trials. When confronted with trials, walk it out and comfort yourself with hope for tomorrow because "this too shall pass."

Day 220   August 8

THE LAZY MAN says, "There's a lion in the street." A stronghold of doubts will prevent you from moving forward in life as you live in excuses. Imaginary problems like lions in the streets will make you live in excuses of why you cannot fulfill your destiny and be successful. "I can do all things through Christ to strengthen me." Keep your feet moving! There is no lion in the street, and you cannot be defeated with God on your side.

"GET BACK TO basics." Sometimes we get so totally engrossed in the flamboyancy of life that we miss the obvious. The basics are all the little keys to success. The small things don't usually carry the fanfare as do the extravagant deeds, so they are often left unchecked and forgotten. These little things are the difference between success and failure. "He who is faithful in the little things will become ruler over much."

Day 221   August 9

SETTLE DOWN AND do not allow stress to rule your life. There will always be disappointments, betrayals, losses, delays, mistakes, deaths, and disagreements, but equal to these common problems is a joy that goes beyond understanding, an excitement about life as we travel this journey that is filled with sweetness, love, successes, blooming flowers, sweet surprises, family, and delightful people. "Think on these things." "As a man thinks, so he is."

CONVICTION IS ACTUALLY a blessing. Even though it is a bad feeling and a rupture in your heart, it is still a gift. "God convicts those he loves." Conviction is the way God turns you away from dangerous, sinful things. Things that will harm you. It is not a punishment but rather a blessing. Do not harden your heart against conviction "for God disciplines the one he loves and chastises his children."

Day 222   August 10

A LACK OF confidence will tank your life! Those with higher levels of confidence are proven to be more successful and less affected by stress and are happier in general. Confidence does not require that you be born rich, beautiful, or talented. Confidence happens by perfecting your faith. Confidence knows and expects God to do what he says, and it draws people to you and brings favor in every area of life. Use your own lot in life to build on. Do the absolute best you can with what you have and who you are. Nothing is too small for God to bring to a place of complete success. "God is faithful to finish the work he has started in you."

PURPOSE IN YOUR heart to leave your past behind. You can't do anything about the things you have done wrong in your past except make a decision to change them from this point forward. God forgives you if you have asked him for forgiveness. Be finished with regret and dread, and move forward. "Forget those things that are behind and look towards those things that are ahead."

Day 223   August 11

WHEN GOD IS your Daddy, his love is never based on your performance. He loves you unconditionally. Your works may please him, but it is not the reason he loves you. Your biological dad may judge you by your abilities, but God is "Father to the fatherless." There is nothing in this whole wide world sweeter than my father-daughter relationship with my heavenly Father. I missed this with my biological daddy, but the deepest longing of my heart has been satisfied by my heavenly Father. Thank you, Lord.

"THE WAYS OF the Lord are right. The righteous walk in them, but transgressors stumble in them." God has laid out a perfect plan for man's life. The wise man attempts to walk in the ways of the Lord, while the fool bumbles along through life, often thinking he's got it all figured out until the fall that is bound to come when you walk outside of God's perimeters.

DAY 224   August 12

ALWAYS REMEMBER THE joy of life is not in the destinations but rather in the journey. Life is filled with all sorts of both good and bad events, but if you can always remember when you are going through a trial that there is something good ahead, it brings a mystery to your journey. Enjoy every step of the journey and don't rush to get where you think you are going. Rather, take the time to enjoy the people and the scenery of every life excursion. And "only concern yourself with the worries of today because tomorrow has enough worries of its own."

EVERY CHOICE YOU make will frame your next decision. Choices are without a doubt the most important part of a successful life. One bad choice can change your life forever. Sometimes we flippantly make decisions without considering the long-term consequences. Be intentional with every single choice that life presents. "I lay before you life and death, blessing and cursing. Choose life."

DAY 225   August 13

GOD OFTEN USES storms and the weather to accomplish his purpose. Look and listen for God in the midst of a storm. His voice is like thunder. "Listen carefully to the thunder of God's voice as it rolls from his mouth." "There will be strange signs in the sun and the moon and the stars. And on earth, nations will be in turmoil, perplexed by the roaring seas and strange tides." Be prepared. I believe our Father in heaven is about to communicate with us through the weather, but he will protect his own. Fear not and listen up.

THE ESSENTIAL MESSAGE of Jesus is that he loves the lost, and his followers should extend that same love. Color, political preferences, financial standings, none of this should matter. We are told to love everyone. You do not even have to like them, but you do have to love them. Prejudice of any kind is an abomination to God. You do not have to hang around with everyone, but you do have to love everyone.

DAY 226   August 14

PERSISTENCE ALWAYS PAYS off. Most times, we don't have victory because we do not persist. Persistence is a very valuable gift. And if you couple persistence with prayer and God's favor, you are unstoppable where men are concerned. And so, how do you get God's favor? By honoring him and always doing what is right. He gives the favor, and you supply the persistence. "If God is for you, who can be against you?"

SELFISHNESS IS DESTRUCTIVE. The antidote is giving. Giving will encourage others, and whatever good thing you do for others, God does for you. He will often use others to bless you, but it is still God. Giving is a sacrifice that opens the windows of heaven on your life. When you are generous, you activate God's blessings, and he "pours out blessings such as you've never seen."

Day 227   August 15

WE ALL HAVE a weak point, and the enemy will always begin his work against you at your weak point. Although we should never focus on our weakness, we need to be aware of them so we can give them special protection. Rename your weak points and start calling out positive changes. "God calls things that are not as though they are." As you speak positive things over your weaknesses, believe that "God is faithful to finish the work he has started in you." Expect breakthroughs in your tweaks.

AGAINST ALL ODDS, we can be successful! "The race does not always go to the swift! If we explore our God given talents and put them outrageously to work, and then make a decision to do something great, success will come! Shoot for the moon, and then work like the dickens towards your goal. "In due season, you shall have your reward."

DAY 228   August 16

SUPERNATURAL INTERVENTION IS an amazing way to get a victory, but most times, we need God's enabling grace to get victory, which requires our physical interaction. A supernatural victory is basically what we call a miracle, as he goes out before us. We don't even need to lift a finger, as he just does it for us. Of course, we are all looking for the supernatural intervention, but most of the time, God includes us in our victory with his enabling grace to do the work. I believe more breakthroughs are lost because people sit around waiting for a miracle instead of getting out there and doing what God has given you the ability to do. "Faith without works is dead."

GOD'S POSTURE TOWARDS sin and wrath is disdainful, but his posture towards the sinner is grace and mercy. "Where sin abounds, much more so does grace." Just like a parent who has a wayward child feels intense sorrow and grief, God sincerely grieves over a lost one. Our posture towards sinners should emulate God's grace. Yes, we hate the sin, but yes, we love the sinner.

Day 229   August 17

MANY PEOPLE SAY they are believers, but just believing is not good enough. Even the devil believes! There is so much more than just believing that God is real. "You will know them by their works." It is not just your verbal confession that makes you a true believer, but it also includes your works. Works alone cannot get you to heaven, but it counts, and when we get to heaven, we will stand before God and be judged for our works. My goal is to hear my God say to me, "Well done, good and faithful servant."

"BE CAREFUL WHEN you think you stand, lest you fall." There is nothing more humbling then when you have been blabbing your mouth about something and judging others, and then you publicly have to deal with it yourself! And this will happen every time. When you choose to judge, it will come back on you like a Mack truck. "As you judge, you will be judged."

Day 230   August 18

GOD TREATS AND loves people he is in covenant with more than those who have not chosen him. God loves everyone, but the true blessings of God will always fall on those who choose him. His desire is that all men would choose him, but unfortunately many do not. God's promises are reserved for those who have chosen him. The principles of God fall on everyone, such as rain and sunshine and the blessing that comes through hard work. But the promises of God are only given to those who make covenant with him, and those promises contain "the keys to the kingdom of heaven," and those keys open the doors to all the real treasures in life.

NO MATTER WHERE you find yourself today and no matter what you are going through, God can and will use you. Your whole life is a mission field. Watch for God, even in the mud and scum of things, because he is always there, and there is always something you can do to make life better for yourself and those around you. Choose to use what you have and where you are to work miracles.

DAY 231   August 19

PRAYER IS SO simple and yet so vital. Live your life knowing that when you pray, you are planting a seed, and many times the seed does not grow in your lifetime but will actually be harvested in the next generation. Never feel your prayers are wasted because you did not see the harvest, but rest assured your prayers are heard, and the harvest will happen. Prayers do not die with people. Your prayers are actually part of the legacy left to your family. "The effectual fervent prayer of a righteous man avails much."

REALITY IS A fact of life. We do not need to deny truth, but just because something appears to be realistic does not make it absolute. Remember God can and will do miracles, even if it goes against natural probabilities. Man's wisdom is foolishness to God and vice versa. God is not limited to the things men have decided is certain. Whose report are you going to believe? I will believe the report of my Lord! How about you?

DAY 232   August 20

"A WISE MAN will hear and increase learning, and a man of understanding will attain wise counsel." Have you noticed how people do not seem to hear the truth? They believe what they want to believe and would rather believe their team than the truth. Always be willing to listen to the logic of something, even if it goes against what you want to be true. "The wise person learns by watching, while the fool has to have a rod taken to his back."

GOD DOES NOT always remove the valleys in your life, but he will bless you in the middle of the valley. God can turn a battlefield into a blessing field! When you're in the valley, it is OK to be honest, but it is not OK to focus or lament over your situation. Let this valley be a learning process. "This too shall pass! Keep going forward. You are almost there!

Day 233   August 21

WHERE THERE IS strife, there is usually misunderstanding, and misunderstanding can easily be settled if we just stop and listen to others. Closed minds create division! Always be willing to at least listen to the opposition. This does not mean you have to agree with them, but usually there will come a certain amount of compassion for their belief if you lend them your ear. We all have a story to tell. "Consider others more important than yourself."

ANXIETY, STRESS, AND worry will eat you up from the inside out. Replace it with focus. Do not allow your mind to meditate on the negative. Be intentional about your thoughts because every action was once a thought. God's Word actually says, "As a man thinks, so he is." Choose your thought wisely. "Whatever things are lovely, pure, right, praiseworthy, noble, admirable, or excellent, think on these things."

GOD IS UNCHANGING. Hold tight to his unchanging hand as you travel this journey we call life. The world and all it stands for is crumbling at an alarming rate, and the road they travel is not only broad and easy to flow along with, but it is destructive beyond words these days. Stay on that straight, narrow path that few will travel, that path that is a holy highway, one which no evil thing may come upon, and one that is filled with beautiful treasures at every turn, and one that eventually leads to our permanent home in heaven.

GOD CAN AND will take the crooked places in your life and make them straight, and incredibly, those crooked places will actually become the highlights of your life because "it is in your weakness that God is made strong." Give your life and all your tweaks over to God. "He is faithful to finish the work he has started in you."

DAY 235   August 23

PERFECT FAITH FOLLOWS God, trusts him, and believes every dash and title in the Word. If God said it, believe it and do it! Follow God, and God will protect, provide, heal, guide, and add all other things to you. "Seek ye first the kingdom of God and his righteousness, and all other things shall be added unto you."

MANY TIMES, YOUR view will affect your vision, and geography and spirituality are often related. A change of pace and place can change everything. A walk on the beach, a hike up a mountain, a scenic drive, all these things can often change a vision. Step back and look at your life from a distance. Many times, "we can't see the forest for the trees." Analyze what you see and ask God to direct you along a path that will lead you to the plan he has for your life. "Acknowledge God in all your ways, and he will direct your path."

DAY 236   August 24

CHOOSE TO LIVE in a respectful manner, no matter how you feel in your heart. Maybe you have been abused and you do not feel like being kind, but always choose to be kind anyway and let your good behavior honor God. This will bring God's favor on you. God knows your heart, and he knows what you've been through. Choose to make the lives of others better than your life has been. Never repay evil for evil and remember "vengeance is mine, says the Lord."

WE SEE SOMETHING, we want something, and then we take it. And that, my friends, is the process of sin. If you are not enamored with Jesus, sin will enamor you, and you will go towards it. Sin is flamboyant, sensational, and so tempting at a glance. Your eyes are your best defense. "Keep your eyes on the things above and not on the things below."

DAY 237   August 25

DISTRACTION IS A ploy of the enemy. Even subtle distractions can pull us away from what we know to be true. There is never a point in your life that you can afford to play into distractions. "Keep your eyes on the things above and not on the things below." There is no substitute for God's Word. And "the enemy is prowling around, seeking whom he may devour." Distraction is one step away from defeat. Stay close to God and do not let distractions pull you away from God.

GOD IS BRINGING about a season of newness. Be expectant and open to embrace the change God has for your life. "Behold, I do a new thing. And shall you not know it? I will make a way in the wilderness and rivers in the desert." If you have felt stuck, be prepared for a new fresh way. Rivers in the desert. Wow. That is nothing short of a miracle. Be prepared.

DAY 238   August 26

NEVER GIVE UP just because you got older, and if you are a young person, never choose to think that just because someone is older, they don't know as much as you do. The Scripture makes it very clear that "gray hair is a sign of wisdom." As we age, we should be teaching the younger people. Titus 2 talks about the older women teaching the younger women. How 'bout we get back to doing that, and let's do it in love? All the days that God has for us on this earth, we should be teaching the younger people.

BALANCE IS THE key to everything in life. When you lose your balance, it will always result in pain. While God wants us to have a full life, too much of anything can throw us out of balance. If you are experiencing discomfort or pain of any kind, stop and rearrange your life to create balance. It works every time. "God loves a just and balanced weight."

"**WE CAN MAKE** our plans, but the Lord determines our steps." It is good to have a vision and to move towards it, but be prepared for changes that may block your way. God promises that he will direct our steps, and they may be different from your plans. Trust that detours are part of his divine plan for you. While it is important to be determined, there is a fine line between determined and stubborn. "Acknowledge God in all your ways and lean not on your own understanding, and he will make your paths straight."

GOD'S CREATED ORDER is designed to run with a particular fuel. God has weighed in on every imaginable subject. And when we choose to go against the way God intended, things will never work at peak performance. The whole universe is groaning because we have chosen to fuel our life by the world's way rather than God's way. "Acknowledge God in all your ways, and he will make your path straight."

DAY 240   August 28

MARK 4:22 SAYS, "For there is nothing hidden which will not be revealed, nor has anything been kept secret but that it should come to light." When it looks like you or someone else is getting by with something, be not deceived because, in due season, God will shine a bright light on all things done in the dark. When we think someone got by with cheating, lying, or breaking any of God's universal laws, it is only temporary. Ultimately, light will always destroy the darkness.

IF SIN WERE completely restrained, we would be in heaven. Don't find it strange when you look around the world and see all the horrible stuff that is going on. It is going to get worse before it gets better, and all we can do is operate in what we know to be right and trust God. "The world is his battle not ours."

Day 241   August 29

THERE ARE MANY who cannot take the heat in the kitchen, and they split at the first sign of trouble. They don't want to get involved, they cannot be depended on when you need them, and they never stick their neck out as they cling to the safe, familiar rock. They never know the thrill of making it through and coming out a winner. They never experience the self-satisfaction of changing a wrong to a right or seeing the positive outcome of a hard-fought battle. They live their lives only concerned about their own comfort and safety, as they follow the passive, apathetic path that leads nowhere and never leaves an impressive legacy. "Run your race as if to win." Quitters never win!

WHEN YOU LOOK to God, he will always give you more than you expect. He will expand your territory and fill your house with treasures. He can make a way when there is no way. He will heal your body and cleanse your soul. He will give you strength, sweet sleep, a satisfied life, and favor with men. What the heck else do you need?

DAY 242   August 30

REBELLION, STUBBORNNESS, AND indepen-
dence are three destructive traits that will block you from
success because they will keep you in a box and alienate
you from God and people. I have people in my life who I
just love who have never prospered because of these
hideous, unproductive traits they hang on to. They are
stuck in their ways, and nothing is going to change their
mind. They are still operating the way their parents did,
even as the world has progressed around them. I call
these people dinosaurs. They are usually know-it-alls,
and as the years go by, they usually become grumpy,
lonely, and intolerable. "The wise man learns by watching,
while the fool has to have a rod taken to his back." Always
stay open to learning!

WE HAVE LOTS of freedom and can still stay in God's
will. The small details are left to our own choices. While
he may be involved in providing a new car, the color and
make is our choice. We have tons of choices, even while
staying in line with his plans for us. Your choices make
the difference between life and death, blessings and cursings. Choose life!

Day 243   August 31

HAVE YOU EVER wondered why some people seem to be more blessed than you or others? Well, it's not your imagination. God really does show favor to some people more than others. He loves everybody, but he responds and shows favor to those who love and respect him. In other words, if you show lots of love and respect to God, he's going to show more love and favor to you! God will respond to and show favor in like degree to those who love and respect him. I don't know about you, but that excites me. I want God's favor in my life, and I am willing to give God the love and respect he deserves. "Blessed is the man who trusts in the Lord and whose hope is the Lord."

IF YOU SAY you believe something, your life should reflect that belief. What you believe should change your life and affect your actions. If you really believe something, it will spark action in the physical realm. Most Americans say they are Christians, but if it doesn't change their life, it is doubtful. If you wonder if someone is a Christian, observe their lifestyle. "You will know them by their works."

September

BRAVERY IS NOT an absence of fear, but it is doing what needs to be done even in the face of fear. A hero is an ordinary person who chooses to step forward and help. Nothing more. Choose to do the impossible. Pray, ask God for help as you praise God, and then move forward and always be ready to be the one who *hits a traitor on the hip or dashes a cup from a perjurer's lip. Be ready to turn a wrong to right and be a hero in the fight.* "Run your race as if to win."

IN HIS PROVIDENCE, God will bring about the perfect result and will do it in his time. Be encouraged: "God has a plan for your life, and it is a good plan, one to prosper you and give you hope and a future." And in that process, we may go through lots of ups and downs and, yes, even doubts. But if you submit to God, every part of the process will work together to bring about that perfect result.

DAY 245   September 2

EVERYONE WILL HAVE seasons of lack in their life. This does not mean God did not hear your prayers, nor does it mean you are being punished. It only means lack happens in everyone's life. Lack can be financial, physical, emotional, spiritual, and even in your relationships. "It rains on the just and the unjust at the same time." Sometimes there is lack that affects many people at one time, or it may just hit you. But I will guarantee you that if you press into God and persist during these times of lack, "he will restore whatever the canker worms have eaten." *This too shall pass.*

IT IS SAID that *seeing is believing*, but I assert to you that *believing is seeing*. In fact, the unbelievers are blinded! They do not have "the keys to the kingdom of heaven" and are not entitled to the inheritance. Believers, never take this magical gift lightly, and when you have a gut feeling about something, trust it. "My sheep shall hear my voice."

Day 246   September 3

GOD SAYS, "IF you look for me, I will be found." If you take one tiny step towards God, he will take a giant step towards you. He says he will be with you in times of trouble, and he will never leave you or forsake you. What a comfort that is to those who believe. While people may come and go in your life, your heavenly Father travels the whole life journey with you. Take that tiny step towards him today and be prepared for the blessings that befall those who seek him.

NOBODY IS PERFECT, yet anything is possible. When a life is submitted to God, the weak become strong, the fearful turn brave, the insecure gain confidence, and the hopeless become filled with hope. No, not perfect, but forgiven and ever growing with the assurance that "God is faithful to finish the work he has started in you."

DAY 247 September 4

DO NOT LET the decisions of others cause you to violate God's Word and your own core values. Use your own set of rules and values and not the man-made rules of others. Just because something is legal does not make it alright, and if it goes against God's Word, you will be judged accordingly! Rules are made by man! "God made man upright, but man devised many schemes." Run everything through God's filter!

GOD'S WISDOM IS foolishness to man, and man's wisdom is foolishness to God. "Check yourself before you wreck yourself." I hear scholars arguing for their wisdom and thumbing their nose at God's wisdom. They will literally be rendered inoperable in due season. The world's wisdom does not work! I don't care how much college you have, if it omits God's Word, it is worthless. "Study to make yourself approved."

Day 248   September 5

"SHOW ME A man skilled in his labor, and he will sit before kings." It doesn't matter what work it is, you can be a ditch digger or trash collector and become extremely successful if you do your job well and are diligent. Many times, I see capable men who are not working because they are holding on to prideful ideas about what kind of work they will accept. If the brook is dry, you have to go where there is water! Many times, God uses small stepping-stones that will lead to great success. "The diligent hand shall rule." Keep your hands moving where you are, with the options set before you!

NEVER LET A negative experience determine your faith. Make a choice to believe God's Word no matter what you may see with your eyes. Always choose to believe in the power of the unseen world because "all things are possible to him who believes." Ask God to help your unbelief. We all struggle with unbelief, but the victorious will choose to push through, as they choose to believe, no matter what. "In due season, you will have your reward."

DAY 249   September 6

JUST BECAUSE YOUR prayer is not answered at once does not mean God has denied it. God has a timing process that must be filled. God's timing is not like our timing. "To God, a thousand years is like a day and a day is like a thousand years." If you have prayed and asked God for something that is within his realm of right, then you can rest assured that "in due season, you shall have your reward."

A CONFIDENT PERSON does not focus on their weakness, but rather they maximize their strengths! When you maximize your strengths, God will take care of your weaknesses. He says, "In your weakness, I am made strong." We spend way too much time fretting over the things we cannot do. Keep your focus on the things you can do and strive to perfect your own unique style.

Day 250   September 7

"YOUR JUDGMENT OF people will come back to you in kind." Be careful when you sling mud around and judge others because you *heard* something! Always remember God's Word is true, and when you judge others, not only will God judge you, but others will judge you as well. We don't get by with anything! It may appear people get by with things for a time, but I promise you, in due season, all things will be judged by God and debts will be paid accordingly. Zip your lip—in layman's terms, shut UP!

YOU CAN DRAW the power of God into your life by eliminating all physical, mental, and spiritual bondages. Anything that draws you away from God will weaken the power of what he can and will do in your life. Distraction is a part of being human. Be intentional about where you let your mind wander. "Keep it on the things above rather than on the things below." This will ensure your success at whatever you endeavor to do.

TYRANTS, MURDERERS, CROOKS, liars, and cheaters may seem invincible for a period of time, but in the end, they will be destroyed. "Yet a little while, and the wicked will disappear. Though you look for them, they will be gone." Don't spend any time fretting over the evil you see prevailing in our country. In due season, God will see that justice is done. Do everything you know to do to help a situation where you might have influence, and then after you've done all you know to do, "stand and believe."

GOD IS GOING to do a new thing. "He will make a way with rivers in the desert." The path God prepares for his children is not always on a flat surface. But it is scalable, and he will walk with you and keep a clear light on the path ahead as he brings provision for the journey. Go in and occupy the land God has prepared for you. Fear not. You got this! "With God, all things are possible."

Day 252   September 9

"**MANY ARE THE** afflictions of the righteous, but the LORD delivers him out of them all." Let's face it, afflictions are such a part of life that no one escapes, but God promises those who serve him that he will deliver them. Keep your thoughts on that as you work your way through the perils of the day. "Though there may be tears at night, joy will come in the morning."

"**WHAT DOES THE** Lord require of you? To do justice, to love kindness, and to walk humbly with your God." It's pretty specific. In other words, to always be fair, no cheating, lying, stealing; to be kind, considerate, and compassionate to everyone; and to not consider yourself more important than you ought and honor and acknowledge God in all that you do, giving thanks in everything and remembering he is your maker, your father, your provider, and your eternal life. Voila!

Day 253   September 10

WE ARE IN a season in our country and in our world where hope is waning. Depression, oppression, fear, unforgiveness, and even suicides are commonplace, and drugs and alcohol are being used to anesthetize the troubled minds. We are told in the Bible that "in this world, you will have trouble," but God is an anchor for our soul to hold us firm and secure in a very shaky world. There is always hope in God. Change your focus to "the things above not on the things below." We always have hope in God.

YOUR FLESH IS a threatening negative force to your life. Your flesh rages against the things of God, and if you allow it to reign, it will always go to the lowest human denominator of life. The way of the world looks so glitzy, beautiful, and tempting, and yet if you just look at the celebrities who succumb to the Hollywood-style life, you will see a huge, enormous number of famous people who divorce, abuse drugs and alcohol, have hundreds of other destructive addictions, and consider suicide. The statistics cannot be denied. The glamour and glitz of the world is a big fat lie! In the end, the things of earth will rust, wither, and die. "Only the things that are done for God will last."

Day 254   September 11

"I AM CONFIDENT I will see the Lord's goodness while I am here in the land of the living." I don't know about you, but I always ask God to bless me in the land of the living. I am not one of those Christians who wants to struggle through life or be a minimalist and live in poverty. I want God's big blessing, and he tells us, "We have not because we ask not." Ask! And then "only believe."

NOBODY MAKES IT through life without a ton of regrets, but it is nonsense to spend time thinking about the things that might have been. The best scenario is to evaluate the errors and make a conviction to not make that same mistake again. We all have skeletons in our closet and things we are not proud of. Embrace your past errors and move on with a renewed understanding of life. "Look to those things that are ahead and forget those things that are behind."

Day 255   September 12

IF YOUR FAITH causes you to mistreat others, you are a heretic and need to change your posture about how you treat others. Your theology is tweaked if you find yourself thinking you are better than others. Love depends on acceptance rather than approval. You do not have to approve of people in order to accept them. "Love others as you love yourself."

RESOLVE IN YOUR heart to always do what is right. A blessing falls on those who do what is right. We instinctively know right from wrong, and our choices should be easy. God will bless your good choices. You may never receive the credit from man, but it will be in your heavenly bank account with God. He sees every single thing that is done, both the good and the bad. "Whatever good thing one man does for another, God does for him." And be not deceived, a curse falls on those who do evil. Nobody gets by with anything!

Day 256   September 13

PEACE IS NOT the absence of conflict. In fact God says, "In this world, you will have trouble." Life is full of challenges, but I love the promise that says, "I will give you a peace that goes beyond understanding. Not like the world gives but only like I can give." It amazes me how calm I have become in the midst of a storm as my faith in God has grown. This promise is for every single person who calls on God to be their Savior. Remind God of this promise when you are tempted to fret.

IF YOU NEVER mourn, you'll never be comforted. Be transparent when you have issues. It is okay to mourn, and it is even healthy. Share your feelings and concerns with others. Find trustworthy friends to share and pray with. "Pray one for the other that you might be healed." When you share, both involved will be healed. It is true a sorrow shared is half a sorrow

DAY 257 September 14

THE POWER OF God's Word is very real, but if it's not spoken with faith, it loses its power. If an atheist who doesn't believe in God's Word decrees something from God's Word but doesn't believe it, it has no power for him. It is your faith coupled with God's Word that will move a mountain. In these troubled times, we need strong faith, and the only way to build your faith is by reading and repeating God's Word. "Faith comes by hearing God's Word."

IT DOESN'T TAKE big things to please people. Most times, small, simple acts of kindness will go a long way. One rose, or even a hand-picked wildflower, means as much as a whole bouquet when given with a loving spirit. Don't put off doing something sweet for someone just because you think you don't have enough money or enough time or you want to wait until you can do something grandiose. Just do something simple and from your heart and watch the results.

DAY 258   September 15

GOD WILL ALWAYS turn his back on pride. Anytime you see someone operating out of pride, you can be sure they are about to take a dive. God says, "Pride comes before destruction." It is natural and even healthy to have a godly pride in things like your children or the gifts God has given you, but you are never to flaunt them or boast as if you're better than others. Remember that just as God gave you these gifts, he can strip them away just as easily. "Be careful when you think you stand, lest you fall."

NOTHING GREAT WILL ever happen without commitments. Indecisiveness is double-minded, and God says if you are double-minded and waiver, you will get nothing from him. Make decisions! Even if you choose wrong, God promises he will direct your path and move you over to the right direction. It takes decisions to solidify life. If you are not willing to commit to things, you will never have anything!

DAY 259   September 16

THE END-OF-LIFE DAYS are hard to understand for the senior who is aging, as well as for family members. The Bible refers to gray hair as being a sign of wisdom and requires that youth should respect and honor their parents. It does not come natural to young people to be intentional about listening to and honoring the elders in their life. And yet the fourth commandment requires us to honor our parents that we may be blessed and live long in the land. The success of your life actually depends on how you honor and obey your elders, and it doesn't even talk about whether they deserve it or not. Just figure out a way to do it, and God will honor you.

WHAT MOST PEOPLE need is rarely what they are looking for. In fact, studies have proven that when we have an allergy to something, we usually have a craving desire for it. Go figure! This is all the more reason why we need to acknowledge God every single day when we wake up. Help me, Jesus, to go towards those things in my life today that will benefit me and glorify you. Amen.

Day 260   September 17

PSALM 64:8 SAYS, "God will make them stumble over their own tongue, and all who see them will flee away." Do not fret over the evil doers or the liars because God will bring judgment down on them. "This is God's battle not ours." It is not wrong to pray that God brings judgment on evil. Remember "what comes around goes around." Everybody will get their just rewards, whether it be good or bad. When you do something good for others, God will do something good for you, and when you do something bad for others, God will see that justice will be done. God is ALWAYS on the side of justice.

A VALLEY DOES not mean you took a wrong turn. In fact, you can't have a miracle unless you have a mess. Be encouraged as you journey through messes, and expect a miracle when you wake up every day. "Though there may be tears at night, joy will come in the morning."

Day 261 September 18

WHEN WE LOSE something in our life, God will always replace it with something else. The problem is, most of the time, we fail to notice the replacement. Instead, we lament over what we lost. Be intentional in recognizing the new things God has put in your life and focus on them because that is where your blessings lie! "A grateful heart always has enough."

THOUGH THE FLESH may wither as the years pass by, your spirit will never wither. In fact, the spirit is growing stronger as you watch your flesh succumb to age. If your attention has been on your flesh throughout your life, aging will become a very depressing, cumbersome process. On the other hand, if you have faithfully served God, there is a promise that tells us, "Your vine will stay green" and your fruit will stay sweet. And I claim that for my flesh. I like it!

DAY 262   September 19

"WHATEVER YOU BIND on earth shall be bound in heaven, and whatever you lose on earth shall be loosed in heaven." This is a mandate God has given to us, but remember mandates from the Lord are conditional depending upon our response. I think this mandate is so powerful and not used nearly enough! Start binding and loosing the evil that is trying to steal our country. Do this in the name of Jesus and then believe.

THERE ARE SEASONS in your life when all you can do is stand on God's Word and make a decision to believe it. The circumstances don't look like it and you don't even feel like it, but all you can do is make a conscious decision to believe it anyway. "Blessed are those who have never seen and yet you still believe." Your choice to believe actually brings a blessing on you.

DAY 263   September 20

I LOVE THE old adage "If something sounds too good to be true, it probably is." It's a wonderful characteristic to be trusting, but God tells us to "be wise as a serpent and gentle as a dove." It is not wrong to be suspicious of things that don't appear to be right, and remember God often gives us a gut feeling about things. It is always a good habit to pay attention to gut feelings when you serve God because, many times, it is God warning us and directing our steps.

DO-OVERS IN LIFE are really not possible. Once something is done, it cannot be undone, but we do have opportunities to rectify our wrongs by learning from our mistakes and choosing another option next time. A sincere apology goes a long way as well. We all make mistakes, and consequences are part of the deal, but if you grow from your mistakes, they have worked towards good, just as promised.

Day 264   September 21

EXTRAORDINARY RISKS WILL bring about extraordinary results. Consequently, ordinary risks bring about ordinary results. It is foolish to think you can lead an ordinary, mundane life, never take risks or stick your neck out, and yet expect to have anything extraordinary. Whatever you put in is all you get out. "Run your race as if to win."

SOMETIMES, WE HAVE to defy the facts as we stand and believe what God said about something. When the circumstances appear to be one way and God says something different, who's report are you going to believe? I'm going to believe the report of the Lord! "Those who put their trust in God will never be disappointed."

DAY 265   September 22

EVEN WHEN EVERYTHING seems sure and logical, still check in with God. Our culture accepts all sorts of things that are offensive to God. Do not fail to check the facts, even when you are positive about something. Just as our culture checks Google, Christians need to check the facts the Bible provides. Our book of life includes an answer and an antidote to everything. Read the Bible!

"GOD PROMISES US peace that goes beyond understanding." This does not mean we will not have problems, but it does mean we will have peace in the midst of the problem. The closer you get to God, the more you know that no matter what happens, everything is going to be OK. There is nothing to compare to the feeling of knowing that, beyond a shadow of a doubt, everything is going to be OK because "those who put their trust in God will never be disappointed." Everything is OK!

Day 266 September 23

IF YOU FORSAKE the Lord, it is your loss. He will still love you, but he will never interfere with your right to choose. God gives every man the choice between life and death, blessing and cursing. Life is a tapestry of events that are intricately woven by your choices. Choose life and blessing. Remember the word blessing means to be happy. Happiness is actually a choice! Wow!

WITHIN THE SACRED picture of life that God has painted for men, you must forgive others, or you will not receive God's mercy and grace. When you choose not to forgive others, you are standing alone without the covering of God. This is a very scary place to find yourself. If you do not release others for their sins against you, God will not release you. I don't know about you, but when I think of it like that, I know I'm going to forgive everyone. I need God's mercy, and so do you. "Those who show mercy will have mercy shown to them."

DAY 267   September 24

WHEN YOU FIGHT against things that are not in God's plan for your life, you will always win if you stand on God's Word. It may take time, and there may be some pain and tears, but if you do not faint, you will win. The key is to stay in the boundaries that are clearly laid out in the Word of God. God will never bless something that is out of his boundaries. Stand strong, fear not, and do not waiver. You got this. "Fret not, it will only cause harm."

OUR BIBLICAL BELIEFS should never interfere with how we treat others. Just because we know something is a sin does not give us the right to mistreat or judge others for their sin. On the contrary, we are to love the unlovable and be moved with compassion. Church should be nothing more than a mosaic of messy people who are loving each other in their sin and believing that "God is faithful to finish the work he has started in all of us."

Day 268   September 25

OUR SIN IS not some little teensy thing. It's huge, and other people's sins are not bigger than yours. Sin is sin is sin, and though some religions differentiate between sins by calling them venial or mortal, this is not scriptural. All sin is grievous to God and all sin is forgivable by God when we ask for forgiveness. Remember that "as you forgive, you are forgiven." We are all sinners, so be kind.

WHEN LIFE HAS dealt you some harsh blows and you are attempting to resurrect your life, the first step to rebuilding is always the first step. Sometimes we don't even know how to begin, and all we can do is take that first step and just walk it out. You simply start, and God will direct your steps if you have acknowledged him and asked for his guidance. And do not back down! Stand strong, and if you are in line with God's Word, you will have success. "Grow not weary of well doing because, in due season, you shall have your reward."

DAY 269   September 26

LIES ARE LIES, and when and if you choose to lie, you open the door to Old Red Ears because he is the father of lies. Sometimes we embellish a story to the point of wild exaggeration, and even though this is socially acceptable, it is actually lying and puts you in jeopardy. The truth is always the best option because every lie, no matter how small, will eventually be uncovered. "All things done in the dark will someday come to light."

FOCUS ON WHO you are rather than who you are not. Everyone has special talents and gifts, and it is completely useless to spend your time lamenting over what you don't have. Take the gifts God has given you and magnify them. Work on enhancing them and use them whenever you can. God will always help you, but you have to do your part. "Before you were formed in the womb, I knew you, and before you were born, I consecrated you." God loves you just as you are.

Day 270   September 27

MOST TIMES, A bomb must be tested to understand its strength. And this is true with men as well. You will never know how strong you are until you have to handle trials. Those who never have to deal with any drama will not be able to speak from experience to help others. The old adage "The iron that has been through the fire is the strongest" is absolutely true. When you find yourself having to deal with negative situations in your life, count it all joy because it is building your character.

THERE ARE TIMES when someone makes a valid point, and yet you feel offended. This offended response is usually rooted in pride, and your refusal and resistance to logic will keep you from growing. Hanging on to your personal opinions that have been replaced by time and progress is downright ignorant. If you don't bend, you will break. "Forget those things that are behind and look towards those things that are ahead." No matter how old you get, keep learning!

DAY 271   September 28

WHENEVER YOU MAKE a change in life, whenever you get a new position or a new adventure, you will often feel inadequate and wary. The human condition wants to *cling to the rock*, cling to those things that are familiar. And ofttimes we miss opportunities because of the fear of change. And yet without change, nothing will ever be different. You'll never reach the pinnacle of success without change. Embrace the change that God is offering and move forward with the confidence that "God directs the steps of the righteous." But you have to move your feet for him to be able to direct your steps. Go for it.

JOY IS THE absence of fear. It doesn't mean you go around giggling. But it does mean that even in the midst of trials, the joy remains. Unlike the temporal happiness that consumerism and stuff bring. This kind of happiness has to be constantly fed with new things and new excitements to remain happy, while joy, along with peace, goes beyond understanding to those who have given their hearts to the Lord.

Day 272   September 29

YOUR VALUE DOES not decrease based on someone's inability to see your worth. Do not allow the opinions or actions of others to make you feel inadequate.
Your own opinion of yourself is also very valuable in your
success as well. God made you special, and you need to
make sure you know and appreciate who you are. Instead
of comparing yourself to others, concentrate on fluffing
up your own special, unique character. "You knitted me
together in my mother's womb. You knew my name
before I was born."

WHEN YOU LIFT others up, you will automatically
rise yourself. If you put perfume on someone, you will get
some on yourself. That is just a fact! Encouragement is a
form of giving. It is more blessed to give than to receive,
and remember blessed means be happy. So giving in all
forms is attached to happiness. That is a powerful statement. Feeling a little low? Try giving.

Day 273   September 30

ARE YOU GOING to memorialize the miseries in your life or the miracles? Don't even share a story unless you have a happy ending to share. A miracle in process always looks hopeless, but that hopelessness is what creates miracles. Be encouraged and expectant that this very thing that looks impossible can have a miraculous outcome. "All things work together for good to him that believes and loves God and is called according to his purpose for him."

EVEN THOUGH GOD is in control, we still play a huge part in what happens to us. Don't get complacent and think, "Oh well, God has this." God is not going to drop pie out of the sky, and he is not going to do your life work for you. Your actions make a huge difference in your life. "God has a good plan for your life, a plan to prosper you and not to harm you." But your mouth and your actions can literally change the good life that God has planned for you. Start claiming what God says about you and then move forward as if you believe it.

October

SPEND YOUR DAYS listening to the song of life rather than daydreaming about days gone by or days yet to come. Every single day has its own special set of beauty and should never be compared to the past or the future. There is beauty everywhere, even in the mundane and the trials. There is a treasure that lies within every trial and within every day. Be expectant and choose to focus and "think on those things that are lovely, beautiful, praiseworthy, and if there be any noble thing, give it your thoughts."

PRIDE WILL CAUSE a person to take the credit for things God and other people deserve, while humility considers God and others first. "Pride will cause destruction," while "the humble will be exalted." Squelch the human tendency to take bows and instead give credit where credit is due. Pride is often rooted in selfishness or unworthiness. Ask God to remove these two destructive lies from your mind and choose to give honor to God and others.

DAY 275   October 2

NOBODY'S PERFECT, AND God loves everyone, and everything is possible with God. Be patient and forgiving to the human frailties of others, just as God is patient with you. We are all full of human tweaks, including you. It is so easy to stand back and critique others and think that you know what they need to do. A better idea is to clean up your own act and make every effort to see the good in others. "God is faithful to finish the work he has started in all of us."

"THE PATH OF the just is like a shining light that shines more and more towards the perfect day." What an amazing promise that is! I have watched my days evolve towards perfection as I have served my Lord, and it isn't because it is void of problems. The world is still raging around me, and yet there is an amazing peace that prevails! I pray this divine perfection on all of you as you press in to get to know your maker in a personal way.

Day 276   October 3

WHEN OTHERS LET us down, we tend to keep track. But God tells us forgive, forget, and move on, and this is not always easy. But remember God knows you're hurt. Ask him to help you forgive because unforgiveness is a cancer that will eat you alive. I have always found that when I am mad at someone, if I stop and make myself feel sorry for that person, I cannot stay mad at them. I might make myself think about how hurt or unhappy they might be, and it helps me to have compassion. Free yourself from the poisoned bondage of unforgiveness by "considering others more important than yourself."

LIVE YOUR DAYS abundantly. Reveling in the here and now. We often waste our precious days focusing on tomorrow or yesterday and miss the joy of the present. God says, "Don't worry about tomorrow because it has enough worries of its own." Anticipate tomorrow with a silent expectancy and only glance at your past as you would through the rearview mirror of your car. Focus your attention on what is happening around you and savor the moment.

Day 277   October 4

WHEN PEOPLE LIE to you, neglect you, cheat you, mistreat you, or abuse you and, worse yet, when they keep doing it over and over, it is difficult to forgive them. But Jesus tells us that if we do not forgive, neither will we be forgiven. Unforgiveness is bondage, and it only hurts you. If you let it go, God will bless you. When you pursue those who have wounded you, God goes with you! God can bring forgiveness through you. Just ask him, then let him. "With God, all things are possible."

WORRY CAN NEVER just be stopped; it must be replaced with something, and that something should be faith and trust in God. "Be anxious for nothing, but in all things, with prayer and supplication, make your requests be made known to God, and the peace that passes all understanding will guard your heart and your mind through Christ Jesus." I feel so sorry for people who do not have the blessed assurance of knowing they have an advocate in God who will take all their troubles, fix them, and then return them as precious jewels. Thank you, Lord.

DAY 278   October 5

WHEN THE STUDENT is ready, the teacher will appear. There is no need to try to teach someone something until they are ready to learn. The old adage "You can lead a horse to water, but you can't make him drink" is absolutely the truth. There is a time and a season that the individual character will be able to receive certain truths. There is a "due season" for everything under the sun, and to push someone before they are ready is like picking green fruit. Be patient with yourself and others and remember "God is faithful to finish the work he has started."

THE LORD MOVES when people pray. God doesn't need people to do things, but he responds to our prayers anyway. Collective prayer can impact the world. The way we treat faith and doubt has a direct impact on our prayers. Doubt can limit what God will do for you, just as faith will increase what God will do for you. Faith activates God! Doubt creates failure in your life. "The effectual fervent prayer of a righteous man avails much."

Day 279   October 6

"**MAY THE LORD** avenge between you and me." In the end, God will avenge. Be at peace and give it to God. The arm of the flesh is vulnerable, but God always wins. "Get rid of all anger and wrath." If you do not deal with anger, it will grow back and get bigger. Sometimes we think we have forgiven but have only dealt with the surface of the unforgiveness. We have to get down to the root and completely eradicate it before we are totally healed. Remember anger and unforgiveness eat away at you like a cancer. Ask God to show you the root, and then deal with it.

A GENEROUS PERSON will always prosper, and when we refresh others, God will refresh us. There are so many ways to be generous: a kind word, a touch, a gift, a smile, a thank you. One of the nicest things we can do for others is to be kind to their human frailties since we all have them. Always be gentle and "consider the other more important than yourself." This will secure gentle boundaries in your own life.

DAY 280   October 7

GOD REMINDS HIS people that we are to "admonish the idle, encourage the fainthearted, and help the weak." I think it would behoove all of us to take that scripture apart and figure out exactly what God was saying. I often hear people say they don't have a ministry. This is a ministry in itself! We are to literally shake our finger in the face of those who are lazy, as we are to do all we can to bolster people up and encourage them, and we are to help the weak whenever we can. What a beautiful ministry!

"YOU WILL SEEK me and find me when you seek me with all your heart." Ever wonder why some people just can't seem to get in touch with God? This scripture answers that question: you have to seek him with all your heart! God is not like a Ouija board or astrology or crystal balls that you can just fiddle around with. He is the powerful, omnipotent Father, and he will never force himself on you. If you want to taste the sweetest thing in the world, "seek him with all your heart, and you will find him."

DAY 281   October 8

"GOD MAKES EVERYTHING beautiful in his own time." When things are all amok in your life and discouragement wants to take hold of you, bring that scripture to mind. As years go by and you look back on life, you will realize the truth of this verse. If you choose to see it, every life scenario holds within it a pearl, something of great value. And usually, the worse the situation, the more beautiful the finish. Be encouraged!

"WHOEVER WALKS WITH the wise becomes wise, but the companion of fools will suffer harm." This warning is from the book of Proverbs, which is full of wise sayings. If you take the time to study Proverbs and apply it, wisdom will abound in your life. Never think you are above the influence of a bad companion. If God tells us to beware of something, we need to take heed. Surround yourself with people who you would like to be like because, in the end, your friends always reflect who you are. "As iron sharpens iron, so the countenance of a friend sharpens a friend."

DAY 282   October 9

THE ORDINARY IS often disguised as God. It is not always the lightning and thunder that represents God. It is not always the obvious, flamboyant miracle but rather the simple, sweet things we take for granted. It's not the loud booming voice but rather that still, quiet voice that whispers in your ear and says, "Stop and go this way." Sometimes the biggest move of God is wrapped up in a very small package. "Give God praise for all things." He is not only the God of the big things, he is Lord over everything. Watch for his treasures throughout your days.

"WORRY IS FUNCTIONAL atheism." When you are worrying, you are acting like you don't think God can handle things. Jesus tells us NOT to worry. This is not because what you are worried about is not important. It is because your worry is not fruitful. Giving it to God is the antidote to worry. "Fret not, it will only cause harm." Take a deep breath and say, "God knows my needs." "Seek first the kingdom of God and his righteousness, and all other things shall be added to you."

DAY 283   October 10

SELFISHNESS WILL ROB your joy. You will never see a happy selfish person. "Do nothing out of selfishness or vain conceit." Humility is a virtue, and true joy will only come when you serve others rather than serving yourself. It is truly "more blessed to give than to receive." I think maturity as a Christian is realized when you actually understand that scripture. If you don't get the truth of this scripture, your growth has a long way to go, but "God is faithful to finish the work he has started in you."

IT IS SAID we should never trust a man who has never suffered. And I believe there is merit to that. "Count it all joy when you go through the fiery trials because it is perfecting you." Those who have never had to deal with trials are usually immature and often tweaked. The trials you overcome are molding your character. Life is filled with bumps, and God promises to see you through them. Put your faith in God because he cares for you.

DAY 284   October 11

SELF-SUFFICIENCY IS A form of spiritual pride. The Scripture says, "I can do all things through Christ who strengthens me." reminding us it is only through Christ that we can do all things. It is only by God's enablement that we can do anything. "Be careful when you think you stand, lest you fall." Self-sufficiency is a wonderful gift, but if it does not include God, it is dangerous!

MANY CHRISTIANS ONLY put on their helmet of salvation and head out down the bunny trail, totally exposed to the world and its destructive ways. God tells us to put on the whole armor of God, including the breastplate of righteousness, belt of truth, shoes of the gospel, shield of faith, and sword of the spirit. To protect yourself from the unseen evil in the world, you must put on every piece of this invisible armor! Read and meditate on Ephesians 6:10–20 and discover exactly what this means.

Day 285   October 12

"IT IS NOT good for man to be alone." We were created to be social animals, and studies have proven people are happier, healthier, and more successful when they are in community with others. We not only have an inherent need for God, but God made us to need and live life with other people. We are supposed to share, laugh, and connect with others. "Two are better than one because they have a good reward for their work." Do your part to make friends!

PEOPLE ARE BETTER together. Help to enhance the strengths of the team of people God has placed around you. "Value others more than yourself." And tap into their strengths. Leadership is not lordship! If God has given you the ability to lead, do it with humility! Eliminate selfish ambition because, in the end, it will isolate and weaken you. True leadership is humble service. "He must become greater, and I must become less." Humility is not thinking less of yourself, it is thinking of yourself less.

Day 286   October 13

"**AND THE PEACE** of God, which surpasses all understanding, will guard your hearts and minds through Christ Jesus." Isn't that scripture just wonderful! We are all looking for peace, and the only way to get true peace is to have Jesus in your heart. What you don't have, you don't miss. People who do not have the Lord in their heart do not have the slightest idea what they are missing. "Taste and see that the Lord is sweet."

WHEN WE ASK God for help, most of the time he guides us and shows us how to help ourselves. we cannot just sit idly by and expect a blessing to fall out of the sky, we are usually involved in the answer to our own prayers. Be proactive and do what you know to do. God says, "After you have done all you know to do, then stand and believe." He also says, "We are blessed according to the work of our hands." If you do not know what else to do, just keep your hands moving, and God will direct.

DAY 287   October 14

PATIENCE IS A must after you have asked God for something. Ask and then trust God. If you will not lose hope and not give up, he will come through! In order to be blessed by God, you have to be willing to wait on God. God will answer even more prayers that you did not think to ask for if you are willing to wait. "Those who wait upon the Lord shall renew their strength, they shall rise up with wings like eagles, they shall run and not grow weary, they shall walk and not faint."

A SACRIFICE IS not a real sacrifice unless it costs you something. When you give out of your abundance, it does not have near the value as when you give out of your need. Just give! Giving is much like planting a garden: what you plant and how much you plant is what you will harvest. And remember that when you give, "with whatever measure you give, it will be measured back to you." Teaspoons, shovels, buckets, or truckloads, your choice!

Day 288   October 15

THERE IS AN innate desire built into every human to be in community with other people. "It is not good for man to be alone." It is healthy to be in community with others. Aloneness will stunt people. Studies have shown infants who are taken care of but not held or loved will be very slow to develop, both physically and emotionally. God tells us, "The countenance of a friend sharpens a friend." No friends, no sharpening! "Woe to him who is alone because he has no one to pick him up when he falls."

THERE IS A time to stop, and there is a time to move forward. Move towards fears rather than running from them. You will intensify fears by giving into them. Move towards them in faith. Go through the fears rather than walking around your fears. "Walk through the valley of the shadow of death." Remember that as you acknowledge God, he will go with you, and with God at your side, you have nothing to fear. "Fear not, it will only cause harm."

DAY 289   October 16

EVERY MAN (AND woman) needs to have a determined purpose. Your purpose is predetermined, and when you seek and acknowledge God, he will direct you towards that purpose. "He works in you to will and to do his good pleasure." His good pleasure is his purpose for you. Men become lost without a purpose and get into trouble or become depressed. Ask God to show you his plan for you. "God has a good plan for your life, a plan to prosper you and not to harm you."

WE OFTEN SETTLE for making a point rather than making a difference! While it is good to stand on what you believe and even important to tell the truth about a subject, before you take an adamant stand on your topic, check your heart and be sure your reason for wanting to say something is not because you just need to be right. Get your heart right, and then what you speak will have the intended impact. "Out of the abundance of the heart, the mouth speaks."

Day 290   October 17

FEAR IS A constant enemy that waits around every corner and tries to grip the heart of all men. Today in our culture, there are lots of things that give good reason for fear. There are over two thousand fears known to mankind, and man has never been able to find a cure. They medicate it and spend hours in a psychiatrist's office trying to root it out, yet millions of people walk around with debilitating fear. God's Word says, "Call unto me, and I will deliver you from all of your fears." This is the only thing that will work, and I know this firsthand. I was riddled with fears at one time. I called to God, and he delivered me. Ask God, and then wait. Little by little, every fear will go, "line by line, step by step. You shall come to me." Yep, this works!

NO ONE GOING through pain should go through things alone! The old adage "A joy shared is twice a joy, and a sorrow shared is half a sorrow" is absolutely correct. Don't choose to do life alone. Be willing to open up and ask for help and also be willing to help others when they ask. "Woe to him who is alone because he has no one to pick him up when he falls." If you are there for others, they will be there for you when you need them.

Day 291   October 18

SHAME IS STRAIGHT from the devil! All God requires for the forgiveness of sin is confession and repentance. We are all sinners, and every one of us has things we could be ashamed of, but if you have confessed and repented, you are forgiven! It is a lack of faith to continue being ashamed after you have repented. Do not allow anyone to put shame on you. Jesus died on the cross for our sins, including yours. Get over it! "There is no condemnation to those who are in Christ Jesus."

PRUNING IS CLEANSING through loss, just as removing a branch from a tree will produce beautiful, new, fresh growth, the same is true when God prunes his people. Pruning can be painful, but it is always productive. You can't put something in a space where there is already something else, so in order to grow, we must remove one thing to receive another. God prunes those he loves. Don't waste your time whining about what you have lost, instead focus on what you have gained.

CONFESS OUT LOUD what you would like to see happen in your life, and as long as it agrees with the Word of God, you will probably get it, unless God has something better. When we confess things out of our mouth and our ears hear it, we will tend to go towards what we hear. And if you think something often enough, it usually comes to pass. God will often use your own voice to communicate with you. Listen to yourself and be intentional when you say something. "The power of life and death is in the tongue."

YOU WILL NEVER feel a life of real purpose until you get your thoughts off yourself and transfer them to God and other people. Looking inward is not only selfish, but it creates all sorts of fears and self-indulgences. You will get a fresh burst of energy when you turn your attention to the things above, where they will always be redirected to the needs of others. "Give what you need because, "whatever you do for others, God will do for you"

DAY 293   October 20

GOD GIVES HIS people the power to enjoy every little, tiny thing in our life. What a wonderful gift! You do not have to have lots of money or stuff or be doing something extravagant to enjoy your life. On the contrary, life is beautiful just the way it is when you serve God. Take note of all the sweet things that surround you, even in the midst of chaos. And always remember what you focus on is what you are feeding. "Whatever is true or sweet or noble or kind, think on these things."

THERE IS NOTHING wrong with choosing to see things through rose-colored glasses. In fact, I think it is the only way to look at everything. The Word says, "Whatever things are pure, lovely, noble, right, true, or of a good report, think on these things." In other words, rose-colored glasses! While it is important to be realistic about things, it is not necessary to see the harshness of everything. Don your rose-colored glasses and enjoy the scenery!

DAY 294   October 21

WE ALL NEED to take charge of our life and stop letting things like cupcakes and pies control our life! Food, money, sex, stuff, they are controlling our lives. If you put up with them, they will keep using you. Sooner or later, you must rise up and take responsibility for your own life. Get mad at these things and tell them, out loud, you are not going to put up with this junk anymore. God's promises belong to those who are willing to fight for them and are willing to take what he has promised. Wishing is not good enough. You must learn who you are in Christ and take what God has promised you. Pitiful or powerful, you can't have both at the same time.

"TO THE FAITHFUL, God shows himself faithful, while to the devious, he shows himself shrewd." Sometimes it may appear a faithful person is not as blessed as one who is living a reckless ungodly life, but "be not deceived, God is not mocked. As a man sows, so shall he reap." Be patient and stand strong, God will never disappoint you. "Don't grow weary of well doing because, in due season, you shall have your reward."

DAY 295 October 22

WHEN YOU LOOK to God, he will always give you more than you expect. He will expand your territory and fill your house with treasures. He can make a way when there is no way. He will heal your body and cleanse your soul. He will give strength sufficient for the day and peace that goes beyond understanding. He is literally a miracle worker when you look to him. Why would you not?

NEVER GO OUT of your house—not even one single day—without asking God to strengthen you and guide your steps. When you get determined in your life to have the things God says you have, something in the spirit realm will rise up and give you the strength to actually do the things you need to do to cause your life to prosper. Ask God every single day for the strength and ability to do what is set before you. Ask him for creative ideas and for favor. "You have not because you ask not."

Day 296   October 23

PRIDE DEFINED MEANS reveling in your own vanity. Pride is thinking more highly of yourself then you ought to. And pride is a very dangerous place to find yourself in. "Pride comes before destruction and a haughty spirit before a fall." Pride often looks so appealing, but if you are operating in this dangerous trait, you are headed for destruction! There is no way around God's principles. If he said it, it is true! Just because it looks like people are getting by with something for a period of time, be assured their time will come. Self-esteem is a good thing and not to be confused with the destruction pride will cause.

"THE WISE MAN hears the Word and puts it into practice. The foolish man hears it and rejects it." The one who rejects it has a house built on sand, and in times of trouble, everything will crumble around him, and he will have nowhere to turn. Meanwhile, the wise man has built his house on the rock that will withstand the trials of life. I find it so sad to see so many people rejecting God as they struggle through life. "The LORD is good, a stronghold in the day of trouble, and he knows who trust in him."

Day 297   October 24

IT IS WONDERFUL to serve God, but don't neglect spending private, personal time with him. If you are not spending that special intimate time with the Lord, your spirit will become dry. You might be doing tons of work for the church, yet you do not have intimate time with God. Feed your spirit, or it will starve to death, just as your flesh would wither without food. A daily dose of nutrition from the Word of God and time spent in prayer will keep your spirit healthy and robust. And remember "the Word of God is healing to all the flesh."

THE ENABLING GRACE of God will give you the power to overcome issues you are dealing with. Troubling things are like mountains in front of you that block your path. He tells us to speak out loud to the mountains in our life and tell them to be removed. Enabling grace gives you peace through the process and smooths and flattens the mountains, enabling you to move forward despite the circumstances.

DAY 298   October 25

THERE IS NOTHING wrong with the ordinary, the simple, the common, the undramatic. Sensationalism is temporal and always demands more and more to satisfy. Many times, we worship the extraordinary rather than the simplicity of Christianity. Continuous, ordinary things that are performed regularly will create awesome and extraordinary outcomes. "If you're faithful with a little, you will become ruler over much."

EVERY ARGUMENT BETWEEN mankind is about who is the greatest. Wars are started, marriages and friendships are broken, families are alienated, churches are divided, all over who is the greatest! Just imagine: wars, divorces, families, friendships, jobs! I find that shocking. The need to be better, smarter, faster, richer in things that are temporal here on earth! A better, healthier way is to "love others as yourself." Imagine a world where we did as Jesus instructed. Competition is an ugly trait rooted in pride, and "pride comes before destruction."

DAY 299   October 26

GOD LOVES MESSY people. You do not have to get cleaned up before you come to God. Just as we love our children even when they are brats, God loves us even bigger. We cannot do anything that will change God's love for us. It does grieve him to see you go amok, just as a parent grieves over a wayward child. It is not by following rules or religious dogma that makes God love you. He loves you unconditionally, and "he wishes that all would be saved."

"NEVER DESPISE THE day of small beginnings." Everyone wants to shoot right to the top, and no one wants to start small, yet this is what God says is the way to do things. Start at the bottom and work up. "Money amassed quickly is quickly lost, but amassed little by little, it has great value." This is true for everything in life. Be willing to start small and grow one brick at a time. "Be faithful with a little, and you will become ruler over much."

DAY 300   October 27

"GOD'S STRENGTH IS made strong in our weakness." Our strengths do not reveal God's power nearly as well as our weaknesses do. Allow and expect God to show himself strong when you feel weak. When you choose to wrestle with God, you must know you are never going to win! Give it up, and give into God because, in the end, your knee is going to bow just like everyone else's. Do it the easy way rather than the hard way!

BELIEVING GOD EXISTS is not the same as a true exposition to the total Bible and turning your life over to God. Even the devil believes God exists. There is a huge percentage of people in our country who would tell you they are a believer. This means they believe there is a God, but having Jesus as your Lord will totally change your life, while believers alone can stay the same all their life with no growth of character. "You will know them by their works." Are you just a believer, or is Jesus your Savior? Huge difference! "As for me and my house, we serve the Lord."

DAY 301   October 28

WHENEVER A PAINFUL situation persists, it is tempting to believe God is not going to answer your prayer. We all have difficulty at one time or another, but one of the good things these difficulties accomplish in us is compassion for others. Being a Christian is not always about everything being perfect. It is about trusting God even in the storms. It's about keeping hope even in the trials of life. If you are going through a trial yourself, pray for someone else who has something going on because the Word says, "Pray one for the other that you might be healed."

REVEAL RATHER THAN conceal. Unhealthy, dysfunctional things grow in the dark. Receive, don't refuse help. Yield to God and don't demand from God. "His grace is sufficient," and there are times your best prayer is for his "enabling grace." There will be times you just have to deal with something, and your success will depend on how you handle these trials. I always claim the promise that says, "And this too shall pass."

DAY 302   October 29

GOD HAS MOVED mountains before, and he will do it again. "Only believe." When you find yourself in a situation where a mountain is in your face, encourage yourself by remembering the things God did in your past, things that seemed impossible. These reminders are faith builders. Another way is to read an account of a miraculous situation in the Bible or recall something God did for one of your friends or family. Never underestimate the power of the testimony, as it will build your faith every time. "We overcome the enemy by the blood of the lamb and the word of our testimony."

IF YOU FREQUENTLY attempt to hide mental pain of any kind, it will increase your burden. It is better to admit to someone what you are feeling and get their comfort and their prayer on your situation. There is power in agreement. When you keep things in the dark, they will magnify. Put light on it. Do not be ashamed of mental pain. It is no different than a physical pain that needs attention. "God did not give us a spirit of fear but of power and love and a sound well-disciplined mind."

DAY 303   October 30

KNOWLEDGE OF WISDOM is not the same as putting action to the word. Better to put action to one scripture you know well than to know the whole Word and not do it. The Word says, "You will know them by their works." There are those who have a theology degree, but it means nothing unless it is activated by a lifestyle. To have something in your head is completely different than having it in your heart. There are those who have wonderful thoughts in their head, but the heart never comes into play, and the issues of life flow from the heart of man.

WE TEND TO want to give God our deficits but not our profits. Many times, when we are doing well, we neglect God, and then when we go amok, we tend to blame God. He tells us to "acknowledge him in all our ways, and he will make our paths straight." Instead of waiting until you have slipped over onto the wrong path, acknowledge him while things are doing well. Every single one of us needs God. Praise him when things are good and trust him through the trials.

DAY 304   October 31

YOU CAN EITHER ask God to give you humility, or he will force it on you, and I guarantee you, it is always more palatable if you ask for it. Find that place in your life where pride has control and give it to God because "pride comes before destruction and a haughty spirit before a fall." Though pride can sometimes appear very handsome, it is really an ugly monster. If you choose to humble yourself, God will be gentle with your growth, like a horse that the rider can gently move with a slight bridle tug. But also like the stubborn horse that must be spurred and yanked to submit, this is like how God will bring his children to submission. Your choice!

I FIRMLY BELIEVE pride has been the nemesis of many well-intending people. The Word clearly says that "pride comes before destruction." Pride happens to be the negative character trait that so many of us tend to fall into without even being aware of it. It is a sneaky wolf in sheep's clothing and can mask itself in many forms. It even ofttimes portrays humility as a cover. Be constantly on guard of this very destructive enemy because it can destroy a life. Be careful that you never make a decision rooted in pride because it will always fail, and it will take you down with it.

November

IF YOU WANT something in life more than you want God, you are out of alignment, and just as the body will hurt when it is out of alignment, so will your life hurt. God should always be first, and you should have a hunger for the spiritual things. Ofttimes we see people seeking spirituality while leaving God out of the equation, but God's Word says, "Seek and you shall find." Be patient with those who appear to be going in the wrong direction. If they are seeking, they will find!!

I LOVE THE "no guts, no glory" idiom, but logically, there is a time to quit! While I think quitters are basically automatic losers, there is a fine line here. My dad, who was a professional boxer, literally got his brains knocked out as he continued to get back up in the ring after being knocked down more times than anyone in the history of professional boxing. While I love the DNA he left his offspring, I think his choice was obviously foolish. When it looks like you should quit, check with God. It might be time to move on.

Day 306   November 2

THE BIBLE IS the greatest book ever written, and it still sells more copies than any other book in the world. While the popularity of contemporary books come and go, the Bible has proven the test of time. The prophecies are accurate, and most are fulfilled, while others are becoming fact right before our eyes. The proverbs and stories are given for life instruction, and it also serves as a book of the history of mankind, profoundly inspired by God himself. Read the Bible. It is your book of instruction!

"IF YOU SET your love upon God, he will deliver you in times of trouble, and if you call on him, he will answer you, set you on high, and honor you with a long, satisfied life." God has given us explicit instructions, and yet we bumble through life, struggling with our own issues instead of putting our trust in him. Trusting God does not mean there will never be problems in your life, but it does mean you will have the best help available as you journey through this troubled world, and you will come out on the other end smelling like a rose!

Day 307   November 3

THE HUMAN MIND has a way of wandering, and things will pop into your head that are contrary to who you really are. There is no condemnation for these random thoughts, but if you entertain these thoughts that are counterproductive, negative, and even vulgar, they will gain power and eventually come to the surface. Remember, everything starts as a thought! The Word says, "Commit your ways to the Lord, and your thoughts will be established." Good thoughts, good life!

THE NUMBER ONE piece of furniture sold in America is the La-Z-Boy recliner. Modern man has a major branding crisis, and it's called lazy! Proverbs says, "A little extra sleep, a little extra folding of the hands to rest, and poverty will sneak up on you like a bandit." No, there's nothing wrong with the La-Z-Boy when it is enjoyed after a fruitful day of work, but way too many people sit in the La-Z-Boy when there is work to be done. Want to get blessed? Get up and get your hands moving. "You are blessed according to the work of your hands."

Day 308   November 4

THERE IS NO denying some people just seem to be more blessed than others, and I do not claim to know the reason for that. But I do know this: God's Word is true, and he says, "I will bless those who have a heart to bless others." There are over six thousand promises in the Bible, and most of them have a caveat attached to them. In other words, God incorporates our choices into the perfection of his will. Choose to do your part to bring about God's promises in your life. Start by blessing others!

ELIMINATE COMPLAINING AND arguing, as they are counterproductive and will destroy your peace and the peace of those around you. There is nothing more annoying than someone who is constantly whining or complaining. Make every effort to see the good in things rather than the negative. If you look for flaws, I guarantee you will find them. But by the same token, if you look for good, you'll find it as well. Spend your days looking for the beauty. "God has made everything beautiful in its time."

Day 309   November 5

TERRIBLE THINGS CAN happen to you even when you serve God. We live in a fallen world, and we are all subject to the same pitfalls. But the good news is, when you serve God, he will see you through everything and strengthen you and make a better, stronger person out of you for having gone through the trial. While those who don't know how to put their trust in God will usually come out of a terrible situation bitter, angry, and weak. "Those who put their trust in God will never be disappointed."

WHEN YOU FIND yourself spiritually in the middle of a dry, weary desert, it does not necessarily mean sin is what brought you there. There are trials that come and go throughout our lifetime, there are ups and downs, and sometimes we win and sometimes we lose. This is all part of the human journey. When things get really tough, it can be hard to connect with God, but there are cool springs and pools of water even in a dry, weary desert. These are the times you really need to push into God. "Draw near to God, and he will draw near to you." God will respond to your call. He will not abandon you in the desert if you stay close to him.

DAY 310   November 6

CHOOSING TO MOVE towards God is a slow process of deliverance. Line by line, step by step, we will inch towards victory. Complete victory does not happen overnight. Sometimes it takes years and even a lifetime to work out the generational curses and kinks in our lives, but as we grow close to him, he grows close to us, and the journey becomes exciting as we leave shackles of sin and the curses that go with them behind. "Grow not weary of well doing because, in due season, you shall have your reward."

WE OFTEN JUDGE others by their worst character trait, while we dismiss our own flaws as trivial. Not fair! The Word tells us to "consider others more important than ourselves." So with whatever mercy you give yourself, you are to be even more gracious to others. Make every effort to see the good in others, keeping in mind that "as you judge, you will be judged." I guarantee you when you judge others, you will have to deal with the very thing you are demeaning. Sometimes it falls on you, or ofttimes it falls on your loved ones and you must deal with it up close. "Be careful when you think you stand, lest you fall."

Day 311   November 7

SOMETIMES GOD SUBTRACTS before he adds, or he takes away before he gives or reduces before he produces. Sometimes he allows us to be backed into a corner or go to the edge of the Red Sea before he opens it. This is all to let you know that it is God who did it. Not you! "Give God glory in everything." You never know when it is his hand that has allowed what you perceive to be a disaster in your life. Stand strong.

"THE PROCESS OF increase always starts with elimination." If your life is cluttered with stuff, the gems will get lost in the shuffle. Weeding out your to-do list should be done daily. Accumulation of things left unchecked will rob your peace and prevent increase. Do the things that need to be done first and be selective about the projects you take on, even though they may be worthy. It is far more commendable to do less and do it well than to ramrod through a bunch of half-baked projects. "A man skilled at his work will sit before kings."

Day 312   November 8

TAKE A STAND against evil and things that are not good. Many times, a position of righteousness will bring about persecution, but the spiritual reward for your dedication and commitment will far outweigh the worldly benefits of compromise. Our country is accepting so many things that are contrary to God, and our consciousness has been seared by the things we are exposed to on television and even in real life. The leaders in our country lie to us and break the law themselves. This does not make it right. Wrong is wrong. Do not be part of this destructive compromise because "God is not mocked. As a man sows, he will reap."

JESUS SAID, "MY Father will honor anyone who serves me." That is an impressive statement, and you know what? I believe it! Honor is defined as privilege, recognition, prestige, merit, pride, and joy. I don't know about you, but I want to walk out this life enjoying all those promised blessings allotted to those who serve Jesus. If you do not serve Jesus, you might want to rethink your position.

Day 313   November 9

PROGRESS IS A key to happiness and success. Keep moving and changing as you go. We were never meant to sit in one place and get stagnant. Just as the world is continuously moving, we need to move and make adjustments and changes, or we will end up in a very small box that is boring and unhealthy. Be willing to change! Be willing to flow with the movement of the culture as long as it stays in line with God's Word. God says, "He directs the steps of the righteous." Steps mean movement. Keep moving!

WHEN WE FEEL anxious, hopeless about the future, bitter, angry, and stressful, we will usually make unhealthy decisions and tend to abandon our faith because it doesn't seem to be working anyway! During these times, it is even more important to hold unswervingly to hope because hope latches onto faith, and without faith, you put distance between you and God, which will weaken you. These times of trial are the times you need to draw on God's wisdom more than ever. Close proximity to God will always strengthen you. "Grow not weary of well doing because, in due season, you shall have your reward."

Day 314   November 10

WHEN THE HEAT gets turned up in your life and things are not going as you want them to go, don't rush to get out of your situation. Instead, try to learn what you are supposed to learn. Everything that happens in our life carries with it a learning curve. If we do not take the time necessary to learn what God intended for us, we will have to do it again. We have all seen those who go through the same trial, over and over, simply because they chose not to learn their lesson. "The wise man learns by watching, while the fool has to have a rod taken unto his back."

ESTABLISH YOURSELF IN unwavering faith by making intentional decisions to trust God, no matter what the circumstances look like. Things can and often change in the blink of an eye. When you are going through tough times, comfort yourself by saying out loud, "And this too shall pass." There is nothing under the sun, whether it is good or bad, that does not evolve and change. Decide ahead of time that no matter what life brings your way, you are going to savor the good times and learn from the trials.

Day 315   November 11

JESUS DID NOT come to condemn the world. He came to save it, and as Christians, that should be our goal as well. Many times, we spin our wheels, judging and condemning the world instead of trying to win them. We will never be able to win anyone to the Lord by judging them and shaking our finger in their face. "It's God's loving kindness working through us that will draw others to repentance." Remember you do not have to approve of someone to accept and love them.

THE THREE MOST important things in your life are your master, your mission, and your mate. Your choice of these three topics will establish your life for good or bad. God, of course, should be your master. Your mission should be a God-given vision that is a noble profession, executed excellently and passionately. And lastly, your mate is who you are yoked with, and that yoking will either lift you up or drag you down. Choose wisely.

SOME OF OUR greatest blessings come from the seemingly bad. Some of the worst things in our life produce the best things in our life. Remember that, as you believe, it is done unto you, so during times of a trial, set your mind to believe this is going to turn into something wonderful. Some things are impossible for men, but "all things are possible with God."

GRACE AND MERCY will always supersede the law. The Old Testament represents the law with the sacrifices and tough restrictions that God realized man could not adhere to. When Jesus came, he fulfilled the law and took everything on himself, leaving us with the New Testament that represents mercy and grace. He reduced the ten comments to two commandments. "Love God with all your heart and soul." And "love your neighbor as yourself." All ten commandments become fulfilled if you adhere to these two. This does not negate the Old Testament. It simply means that if Jesus changed something at the cross, it does not come through into the New Testament. Mercy and grace were introduced. Proverbs, Psalms, and all the history and prophecies still stand. It is important to get to know both testaments.

DAY 317   November 13

GOSSIP IS AN accepted form of abuse! There are times we feel we will burst if we don't say something about someone that is eating at us. Yet if we hold it in, it becomes hidden anger, and we react negatively. It is important that we get it out, but we need to go to God and tell him everything we are feeling. It is not only OK to tattle on someone to God, but it is healthy. He is our Father, and it is fine to take your grievances about others to him. But then we are told to "pray for those who spitefully use us." Ask God to help you forgive them and leave your burden with him. He will handle the problem if you let him. You might lose if you battle it your way. "But those who put their trust in God will never be disappointed."

"THERE IS NO wisdom, no power, and no counsel that can stand against God." It may appear men are getting by with thumbing their nose at God, but rest assured that, in due season, they will have their reward, and it will not be good. The arm of the flesh is so puny compared to God. So "if God is before you, who can be against you?" If you are truly serving God and letting him reign in your life, "no weapon formed against you will prosper."

DAY 318   November 14

BE COGNIZANT OF the thoughts you allow to roost in your head. Just because you can't see something or others can't see it doesn't mean it doesn't have power. We bathe daily to keep our outside clean, and we should make the same effort with the whole body, inside and out. Remember whatever goes on inside of you will eventually bubble to the surface. God looks at the heart of man. "Create in me a clean heart, O Lord."

WE ALL LOVE to find treasures, and God says he will "show you hidden treasures in secret places." Treasures are usually right under your nose, and they are not just literal. They come in many forms: spiritual, financial, relational, physical, and emotional, as well as literal STUFF! We get so busy looking for the treasures way out there somewhere that we miss the beauty of what God has surrounded us with. Within the boundaries of our own lives lie most of our treasures. My mama used to say, "Keep your eyes glued to the ground because you never know what you'll find at your feet." Yep, it's usually right under your nose!

Day 319   November 15

THE WHISPERS OF the world will always lie to you, and the world will never understand the Word of God. In fact, the world thinks God's Word is foolishness or a fairytale, while God thinks "the wisdom of man is foolishness." God says, "The reading of many books is wearisome to the flesh." And he also says, "The Word of God is healing to all the flesh." This does not mean school and study is wrong; it simply means there is way more value in the Word of God than in the books of men. Keep a healthy balance between worldly literature and God's Word.

MOST OF THE time when we say we *can't* do something, we really mean we *won't* do it! The word can't gives us an excuse to not have to do something. Be honest with yourself and others. Can't is rarely the right word! "I can do all things through Christ who strengthens me." Life will be boring and mundane if you are not willing to try something new. Always be open to new ideas. It keeps you young.

Day 320   November 16

THERAPISTS HAVE FOUND gratitude is the healthiest choice you can make. An attitude of gratitude will change your life. There are always things in life you don't have, things to hope for, but I promise you that when you truly appreciate what you have, God will give you more. "Delight yourself in the Lord, and he will give you the desires of your heart." Delighting yourself in the Lord is simply appreciating him and all he has done for you. "Seek first the kingdom of God and his righteousness, and all other things shall be added unto you."

YOUR SIN WILL find you out. it is foolish to think you can get away with sin because "everything done in the dark will someday come to light." There is no exception to God's rules. "Has he not said it, and will he not do it?" Just because it seems you got away with something for a short period of time, be prepared because the light will go on. "As you sow, you will reap." Whatever you sow in your life will produce a harvest, and sin is planting a fruitless, hopeless harvest of weeds that will choke out all the good in your life. "The wage of sin is death."

DAY 321   November 17

LOOKING BACK AND spending time reminiscing will only serve to distract you and get you off course. Identify your destination and keep it in mind as you continue your journey. Train your mind to stay focused on the things at hand and don't be too dogmatic about your days. Leave room for exciting, impulsive excursions that are sure to pop up. Some of the sweetest memories in life are unplanned and unexpected. Enjoy the moment as you "forget the things that are behind and focus on the things that are ahead."

THE KEY TO living a successful life is knowing what to let go of and what to keep. Many times, we cling to the things creating the problems in our life. Things become familiar to us, and even though they are not good, they are comfortable. It is wise to stop every once in a while and assess your life, examining all the aspects that make up your days. Take note of the value of each thing, and just as you would throw out an old ugly chair, throw out the nonproductive things. And make room for the new things God wants to give you. "Forget those things that are behind so you can look forward to those things that are ahead."

DAY 322   November 18

MOST DREAMS THAT are not fulfilled are because of procrastination. It is the number one reason why a person dies with regrets. It is the reason we miss out on life and overlook opportunities. It will cause all sorts of trouble and fill your life with unfinished projects and chaos. "He who hesitates is lost." Procrastination will become a way of life, and the more you do it, the worse it will get. Do not give into this destructive decision. "The hand of the diligent shall rule."

WHAT YOU ARE lacking in the spiritual realm will reflect in your natural life. The spiritual realm, though unseen, is very real, and there are things that need to be addressed if the natural body is to remain healthy. Medical doctors have proven the problems that surface in the natural body are directly related to what's going on inside a person and vice versa. When you see someone who is a mess outside, they are a mess inside as well. Just as we wash and clean our natural bodies daily, wash your spirit with the cleansing Word of God. "It is healing to all the flesh."

DAY 323   November 19

JUST BECAUSE YOUR faith waivers and fails for a season does not mean you are not saved. This happens at one time or another to most believers. Be encouraged and draw near to God, and he will draw near to you. Just because you do not feel God is near you does not mean he is not there. "I will never leave you or forsake you."

THERE ARE THREE levels of intensity of prayer. Ask and keep on asking: this prayer is generally personal and usually includes a petition for something for yourself. It can almost seem flippant, but it does produce results. A little deeper prayer is when we seek and keep seeking. This usually includes a continuous petition for something very heartfelt and usually something for someone we love. Then there is a prayer of supplication, a knocking that is more intense. It is the deepest intensity of all, and this is called intercession. It is when we stand in the gap for someone else. During this intense prayer, we can often feel the sorrow of whom we are praying for. All three levels of prayer are productive. "Ask and it shall be given to you; seek and you shall find; knock and it shall be opened unto you."

Day 324   November 20

WORDS ARE SO powerful! Love is communicated with words, and wars are started with words. Lives are shattered or healed with words. Words are the greatest conduit of power and authority in this world. How are you using your words? Are you using them to build up lives, or are you using them to rip people to shreds? Are you using them to encourage yourself and others? Always remember the greatest power that God gave us was our tongue. Within it lies the power of life and death, and it can "set your life on a course of destruction." Use your words wisely.

TRUST IS NOT a passive state of mind. It is an act of the soul by which we choose to lay hold of the promises of God and cling to them despite adversity. It can be difficult to trust in something we cannot see, but God's Word says, "Blessed are those who have never seen but still believe." So just choosing to believe brings a blessing down on us. Circumstances do not change God's Word, and he tells us hundreds of times in the Bible to "only believe."

Day 325   November 21

DISCOURAGEMENT CAN TOTALLY distract you from what is important in your life. There is never a reason to be discouraged if you truly trust God. Every event in your life will lead to your God-given destiny when you are looking to God. "Grow not weary of well doing because, in due season, you shall have your reward." Growing weary is discouragement. Stir yourself up and keep moving forward.

I OFTEN HEAR people say they can't hear God, or they question things about him and even question his Word. The truth is you cannot haphazardly or flippantly find God. He clearly tells us, "You will seek me and find me when you seek me with all of your heart." If you want to get to know God and enjoy the blessings and promises he gives to those who call him Lord, spend time with him and seek him with all your heart. "Taste and see that he is good." There is nothing sweeter!

DIGGING INTO GOD'S Word is how you find the hidden treasures in the dark, secret places. It is not just by glancing at the Word but rather reading in depth, similar to seeking a physical buried treasure. You don't just skim the surface. You dig deep. That is where you will find the "hidden treasures in secret places." DIG!

"NO GOOD THING will be withheld from those who walk uprightly before God." I love that promise. No good thing will be withheld! And then the last part that says from "those who walk uprightly." Keep in mind that none of us walk a perfectly upright life. We are all sinners in one way or another. Do not let those words discourage you. If you have submitted your life to God, then this wonderful promise belongs to you. Expect good things.

DAY 327   November 23

NEVER SAY YOU cannot forgive someone. This is not an accurate statement. The word is not can't, but it is rather won't. If you can consistently forgive, I promise that one day, you will be incredibly loved. This is a promise from God. He knows when you've been hurt, and he sees your heart. If you are having trouble forgiving someone, ask God to put that forgiveness in your heart. And then just say out loud, "I forgive so-and-so," then do not let yourself dwell on anything that happened in the past. "Forgive and you will be forgiven."

"I WILL BRING light to those things hidden in the darkness." Don't hold back in asking God to enlighten you or show you things that are not easily seen or understood. God promises he will show us "hidden treasures in secret places," and he will "put a light on our path." Ask him to help you stretch your budget, give you creative ideas, direct your steps, and anything else the day throws at you. Put it all in God's hands. "His yoke is easy, and his burden is light."

DAY 328   November 24

PAUSE AND LOOK back on your life and give thanks for all he has done for you. We should not just give thanks on Thanksgiving, but we should be giving thanks every day of our life as we revel in our health, our family and friends, the freedom we enjoy in our country, clean air and water, a roof over our head, and everything else in our life. "Give thanks in everything." Your thanks will open the windows of heaven in your life. "Let everything that has breath praise the Lord." Our God is so good, and I want to give God special thanks today and every day for his grace and mercy. Even when things are not happening right around us, we can always look out and see the beauty God does in other places. There is always a reason to thank God. Happy Thanksgiving.

THERE IS A big difference between attraction and action. Being attracted to something is a huge difference from taking action. Being attracted to something that is not pleasing to God is not a sin. In fact, it is common among human beings. But attraction should never determine your choices. Rather, always check your core values before making choices. "I lay before you life and death, blessing and cursing. Choose life."

FEAR TENDS TO make us skeptical and doubtful and causes us to appear selfish. Fear will cause one to be stubborn and resist change, becoming short-sighted, and prefer slavery over the unfamiliar. Some will not even accept help or change because they are fearful and uncertain. They may appear stubborn and stiff-necked when they are fearful. Getting to know God will gradually overpower fear. Stand firm and allow God to heal you. "Be still and know that I am God." Do not run from your fears. Stand firm and watch God work in your life.

WE RARELY COMPLETELY agree with anyone. It is imperative we learn to agree to disagree with others, or we will be in a continuous battle with the world. Always be respectful of the opinions of others, even when they oppose yours. It is always nice to have a circle around you that is like-minded, but remember that "as iron sharpens iron, the countenance of a friend sharpens a friend." There is nothing wrong with robust dialogue as we glean from each other's opinions. But remember to "consider others more important than yourself." This is the one scripture that will always help us get along with others.

DAY 330   November 26

THE WORLD IS growing increasingly dark, and our world is desperately in need of light. "It is God's loving kindness working through you that draws them to repentance." Judging and pointing fingers is part of the problem rather than part of the solution. Your speech should always be gracious, and we should make every effort to build bridges, even when we disagree with people. People will never listen to you until you are willing to honor their beliefs. This does not mean you have to agree with them, but you need to honor their right to choose. Keep reminding yourself, "This is God's battle not mine!" Don't worry, in the end, he wins!

THERE IS A poem written by Ralph Waldo Emerson, and I felt compelled to memorize it years ago. The main line said, "In the mud and scum of things, there always, always, something sings." The theory is that no matter what happens in life, if you look deep enough, you can find something good within the dark and meanest things. Don't take this line glibly, but really look to find a "hidden treasure in dark secret places."

Day 331   November 27

IT IS EASY to have faith in the beginning and in the end, but where faith is really tried and tested is in the middle. Even though we trust and believe our prayers have been heard, we never know exactly how long it will take for the answer to come to fruition. I have had prayers answered that took twenty years, and it can be hard to remain constant in your faith, but there is a time and season for everything under the sun. If you are believing God for something, never give up because, in due season, you shall have your reward. "Has he not said it, and will he not do it?"

"CREATE IN ME a clean heart and renew a right spirit within me." Freedom happens when we surrender to God and ask him to help and change us. Redemption will only happen when we are willing to submit to God. We cannot be redeemed until we are willing to give control over to God. As long as you hang on to the need to be in control, you will be on your own. God will never force himself on you. Redemption was provided for us by God, through Jesus. The choice to receive this gift is yours. "Choose life."

Day 332 November 28

YOUR ATTITUDE SHOULD be controlled by your conviction, not your circumstances. As long as you allow your circumstances to control your life, you will be miserable. Circumstances are as fickle as the wind, good and bad things come at you with equal velocity, and with them at the helm, your emotions will go up and down like a roller coaster. A conviction is a fixed or firm belief. Find a promise in the Bible and fix your belief on it, no matter what your circumstances look like. I love the one that says, "All things work together for good to those who believe and love God and are called according to his purpose for them." I remind myself of that, no matter what comes at me in life.

NEVER, NEVER GIVE up on God. Though there may be days when it seems like things aren't working, when you feel weary and discouraged, his plan for you has not changed. His plan is bubbling and alive, though it may not be in your scope of vision. Do everything you can within your ability to bring your vision to pass, move forward gently but firmly, and trust the process. "Winners never quit, and quitters never win!"

Day 333   November 29

"**WHEN YOU DO** evil to someone who has done nothing but good to you, evil will never depart from your house." I don't know about you, but I find that scripture to be downright frightening. Search your heart and rid yourself of any wrongdoing you have done to someone who has always treated you good. We have all said or done things that were insensitive, and many times it was not done to offend. Taking offense is both carnal and immature. Don't hold a grudge or try to get even, as it only hurts you! "As you forgive, you are forgiven."

GOD IS AWESTRUCK with generosity. "He loves a cheerful giver." If you find yourself degrading churches for taking or mentioning offerings, you are shooting yourself in the foot. Giving is an honor and a form of worship and always produces a harvest. It is definitely "more blessed to give than to receive." I believe getting hold of this single verse is the first sign of a heart submitted to God: "For where your treasure is, therein lies your heart also."

DAY 334   November 30

DON'T TRY TO police the behavior of nonbelievers. We are judged by what we know, and nonbelievers are not able to see the error in a lot of things. The Word says they are blinded, and I remember very well the years before I knew the Lord. I sincerely did not realize some of the things I did were offensive to God. Be kind to those who do not know any better and set the example by your lifestyle. "It is your chaste behavior that will draw them to repentance," not the shaking of your finger in their face or beating them over the head with your Bible. Not!

"WHEN YOU DO good, you put to silence the ignorance of foolish men." Don't give the foolish anything to talk about. Always choose to do what is right because you are representing your Father in heaven. This, however, does not mean you will please everyone because there will always be people who will find something wrong with you. But when you get to a place where you know you are doing what is right and you are looking to please God rather than man, the ignorance of men will not matter to you.

December

GOD'S WORD IS accumulative and permanent, and "it is sharper than a two-edged sword." I often hear people say they have read the Bible, but I can tell by their conversation and their lifestyle that they have probably only opened the Word of God and read a few verses. The Word needs to be read in its entirety, over and over, because every time you read it, you find a new treasure and your life will begin to change. You never read the Bible once and then say you are done. It is a lifelong journey. "Study to make yourself approved."

STUDIES HAVE PROVEN a huge percentage of people have a desire to read the Bible. It is amazing to me that people do not bother to read this incredible book of instruction. I challenge you to read your book of instruction!

DAY 336 — December 2

LET'S FACE IT, some days you just feel better than other days. Life is so full of ups and downs, and the flesh is so subject to radical feelings. I love the scripture that says, "Though there may be tears at night, joy will come in the morning." Remind yourself of that scripture as you go to bed after a rough day, and expect God to fulfill his Word. You only get what you are expecting. Rise every day with gratitude in your heart and an expectancy of a fresh new day filled with the wonders of life. "This is the day the Lord has made; I will rejoice and be glad in it."

"THE GATES OF hell will not prevail against the church." The gates of hell are any place where there is a concentration of influence. Just as there is power in agreement with the things of God, there's also power in agreement of something evil. A culture can create the gates of hell, but as long as we don't fall into agreement, we are protected. The world is very dark and in great need of our light, even though they don't realize it. This is God's battle. Stay under God's protective umbrella by honoring his Word, and the gates of hell will not prevail against you.

DAY 337   December 3

MANY TIMES, WE get so busy looking "out there" for our blessing, we miss what is right under our feet! Most of the time, you already have what you need to enhance your life. It doesn't require new stuff, new friends, a new husband, or a new house. It requires appreciation and a little TLC with what you already have. When you max out what you already have, God will give you increase! This goes for everything. "If you're faithful with a little, you will get a lot."

IT IS SO grievous to see the lack of compassion that permeates our culture. Grace is threatening to religious folk! They want to see people punished who do not agree with God or them. I have often found myself wishing God would zap someone! Wow, this is so wrong! "When Jesus looked at the masses, he was moved with compassion." As they were crucifying him, he said, "Forgive them, Father, for they know not what they do." As Christians, we are called to shine our light on nonbelievers, show them compassion, love them in their sin, and let God do the rest. "It is God's loving kindness working through you that draws them to repentance."

DAY 338   December 4

"**HE WILL NOT** be afraid of evil tidings because his heart is steadfast as he trusts in the Lord." So what do you care what people think or say! If you are truly putting your trust in God, your heart should be steadfast and confident! To fret over what people might say or think about you is just a plain old lack of trust in your Father, who is directing your steps and has uniquely created you. Make an intentional effort to care more about what God thinks of you than what man thinks of you. This will solidify your strength and confirm your well-being.

NEVER COMPETE WITH your family, friends, or your team! "A house divided will fall." When you encourage those people who God has surrounded you with and you help them, you are strengthening yourself. It is ridiculous to think you can do life alone. There is strength in numbers, and agreement is so powerful that it can move mountains. Get in agreement with your life's team and help them become all they can be. In so doing, you will shoot right to the top.

Day 339   December 5

IT IS POSSIBLE to live in unity even in a deeply divided world. Unity is not necessarily agreement, and it is not the same thing as conformity. It is simply respecting and accepting the differences in others. There are all sorts of reasons why people divide: cultural, racial, political, religious, financial. We do not have to agree with others to remain in unity with them. Differences in opinions should not separate families, friends, churches, or countries. It is rare to be one hundred percent in agreement with anyone. "Be kind and compassionate to one another, forgiving each other just as Christ forgave you."

PURPOSE AND PASSION go together. If you are not passionate about creating, you are just a consumer, and the joy of life is experienced in purpose and passion, not in consuming. While it is fun to consume, it is empty and nonproductive. God placed a need to create in all of us. We are created in the image of God, and he is the master creator and called his creation "very good." The sum of our life should be a collage of created legacies, paving the way for upcoming generations.

DAY 340   December 6

WORRIED OR STRESSED, the secret to good life relationships and successful life experiences is a good response to bad news. Face problems joyfully because problems are inevitable, and how you handle them will determine the outcome. It is not always easy to be joyful in negative situations, but it is said that it takes a lot less energy to smile than to frown. Make a determined decision that you are going to be known as someone who is part of the solution rather than part of the problem. Comfort yourself and others in the throes of a problem with this wonderful promise: "Weeping may endure for a night, but joy comes in the morning."

WHEN YOU TAKE a step out of the ordinary, when you decide to take a chance on something that scares you, when you decide it's OK to think of yourself as being special, that's called courageous, and that's when God can use you in a way you never dreamed possible. It is only men and your own mind that puts limitations on what God has for you. Put your trust in him and go forward in this life, knowing and believing there is a special purpose for you. "God has a good plan for you, a plan to prosper you and not to harm you, a plan to give you hope and a future."

Day 341   December 7

GOD WILL USE the fruit that comes out of your failure to minister to others. Share your testimony of failure and restoration with others. "We overcome the enemy by the word of our testimony and the blood of the lamb." When we have traveled a treacherous journey through life and have overcome, that can be so encouraging to those who come behind you. Share your story with others and help to encourage their walk. I firmly believe encouragement is one of the most profound motivators. Encourage!

WHEN YOU FIND yourself struggling with your identity, remember God chose you if you call him your Lord. What more identity do you need? A child of the most-high God, never forsaken, loved unconditionally, redeemed, forgiven, and made in the image of God. Though men may see you through carnal eyes, your Father in heaven sees you as his perfect creation. Hold your head high. "There is, therefore, no condemnation to those who are in Christ Jesus." Hallelujah!

DAY 342   December 8

FACE YOUR LIFE courageously and fearlessly. Courage means to stand for one's convictions and beliefs, especially in spite of criticism. Courage is moving forward even when you are afraid or it isn't politically correct. Stand firm on what you know to be true and don't be discouraged by the naysayers. Taking a passive stand when it doesn't affect you personally is like letting a fire burn out of control because it is not near you. It will eventually burn to your back door! When you know something is wrong, "Defend the rights of the poor and needy." And "Be strong and courageous."

"IF IT IS possible, as much as depends on you, live in peace with all men." Notice that the scripture says "if it is possible." There are times someone is not willing to be at peace with you. In this case, you are not held responsible. You simply do your part to make peace, and that puts the ball in their court, and they will have to deal with the consequences of unforgiveness. The key is to be sure your heart is right and you have done everything you know to do to bring about peace. "God has called us to a life of peace." There are some folks you just need to love from a distance.

Day 343   December 9

VANITY IS DEFINED as excessive pride or admiration of one's own appearance or achievements, but interestingly, the word also means useless. There is absolutely no value in vanity! It is useless and a waste of time, and generally when you spend too much time focusing on your own attributes, you will find they fade quicker. Those who gloat and puff themselves up are often the first to wane and wither. While it is wonderful to be confident and to be pleased with the way God has made you, "don't consider yourself more highly than you are ought."

HAVE CONFIDENCE WHEN you pray that God does hear you and then never, never, never give up! "If you waver, you get nothing from God." It doesn't matter what the circumstances look like, it doesn't matter what other people think or say, if you have prayed in line with God's Word, then remind him of what his Word says, and then stand and believe. It may take more time to get your answer than you thought, but if you stand and believe, you will receive! "Has he not said it, and will he not do it?" "Only believe."

DAY 344   December 10

BE THE KIND of mate, partner, friend, parent, or sibling that is willing to do whatever it takes to push others over the finish line. Don't be a quitter and give up on the people in your life because God is a finisher, and "he's faithful to finish the work he has started in them." God put certain people in your life for a reason. You can't help the whole world, but you can help those who are within your sphere of influence. Stand in there and encourage, push, and pray for your people. I love the saying that says, "Bad people need to be good, and good people need to be nice."

MANY TIMES, YOU have to go through a wilderness experience in order to find your path to success. It is rarely in your high seasons that you find your true calling, but rather in those low, uncertain times that God will be made big in your life, and he will be able to direct your shaky path. "In your weakness, God is made strong." Sometimes all you can do is just walk it out, even if it is baby steps, trusting God as you go.

DAY 345   December 11

WHEN YOU DECIDE to partner with people even when they are not perfect, you are unleashing true Christianity and generosity that will impact your whole sphere of influence. People will not listen to you by shouting and pointing fingers but rather by how you conduct your own life and how you react when things go amok. "Be all things to all people that you may win some to the Lord."

FIGHTS AND ARGUMENTS happen even with pastors and the rest of the church because we are all human and imperfect, and sometimes a good fight will clear the air and make things better. It is better to bicker than to hold a grudge because eventually the grudge will surface in negative and sometimes subliminal ways that will cause even more problems. Just remember to fight fair and listen to your opponent, and "consider the other more important than yourself."

DAY 346   December 12

SHOW ME YOUR friends, and I'll show you your future. "Be not deceived, bad company corrupts good behavior." Godly, healthy friendships and partnerships are not only healthy, but they are also powerful, and total agreement in prayer with a like-minded person can move mountains. There is an adage that says, "If you want to go fast, go alone. But if you want to go far, go together." Another says, "One sets a thousand to flight while two sets ten thousand to flight." Don't choose to do life alone, but choose your friends wisely.

THERE ARE FIVE major things that will weaken your life and rob your joy: discouragement, selfishness, past regrets, unforgiveness, and anxiety and fear. God gives an antidote for all these destructive, learned behavioral patterns. There is no substitute for real joy other than the Lord. Happiness is not to be confused with joy. Happiness is a temporary state of well-being and can flee in a moment's time when things go amok in your life. Joy is a permanent attitude of the heart that is present even during trials, and only God can provide true joy. "The joy of the Lord is your strength."

DAY 347 December 13

GUILT, GRIEF, AND grudges will not only stifle the joy in your life, but they are also toxic and will poison your whole body. Although there is a time to grieve, even a time to feel remorseful about things you regret, maybe feel a little resentful because someone has wronged you, and it is even OK to experience it for a short time, but then let it go and move on. Never wallow in guilt, grief, or grudges. Begin each new day with a fresh acceptance of the past and with new expectations for the future. "Forget those things that are behind, and look forward to those things that are ahead."

FEAR AND ANXIETY are crippling millions of Americans! I find it so amazing that people will try everything before they try God! I know because I was crippled with fear for forty-one years before I tried God. Until I gave my heart to the Lord and called unto him, I was riddled with fear. Today, God has truly delivered me from all my fears, and I stand here a strong woman who only fears not pleasing God. "Call unto me, and I will deliver you from all your fears."

Day 348   December 14

YOUR PAST WILL never take you where you want to go. Release your past and do not define your future by things that have happened to you in the past or the guilt you feel because of things you have done in the past. If you have asked God for forgiveness, "he does not even remember your sin anymore." It is unproductive and unhealthy to hang on to past regrets. "God is faithful to finish the good work he has started in you." Do not judge yourself by past mistakes. Every morning begins a clean slate, and you can write on it whatever you choose for this day.

"JUDGMENT IS WITHOUT mercy to the one who has shown no mercy." If you choose to judge others, you are shooting yourself in the foot! Every single one of us is flawed, and we all need God's mercy and grace. If we do not give it to others, God will not give it to us. The human tendency is to sit in judgment of others, but God says he is the judge, and our job is to be as kind to others' human frailties as you would like them to be to yours. "Love others as you love yourself."

Day 349 December 15

TWO PEOPLE CAN have the exact same problem in their life, and yet one comes out better, while the other comes out bitter. The one who comes out better is the one who is trusting God and looking for divine providence in their situation, while the other one is lamenting and fretting over the problem and trying to solve it with the arm of the flesh. When you mess up in life, God can and will use your mistakes to work towards good, but you have to believe he can, and you have to let him! "All things work together for good to those who believe God and are called according to his purpose for them."

GOD TELLS US to "bring him in remembrance of his Word." But if you don't know what his Word says, you can't remind him. This is not because he does not know what it says, but he wants to know that you know what it says. It is not disrespectful to remind God of what he has promised us. In fact, he instructs us to do this. It is powerful to call out God's promise when you are praying. If you pray the Word, you bring God into agreement with you, and that kind of prayer will move mountains. Read the Word and learn what God has promised and then remind him. "You have not because you ask not."

Day 350   December 16

THINGS ARE NOT always what they seem. Just because you see something a certain way does not make it so. There are always things that are not seen by the eye that motivate life. Keep your mind open. The only thing that is absolutely true and will never change is God's Word. Everything else is suspect. "The Word is the same yesterday, today, and tomorrow." "Those who put their trust in God and his Word will never be disappointed."

EVEN THOUGH GOD made our brains in such a way that they are the greatest computer on earth, like a computer, they only spit out what you feed into them. The greatest minds on earth can be totally corrupted with trash and afflicted with a virus that can cause the whole computer to crash. Be specific about what you feed your brain because it is "trash in, trash out." Feed your mind good, beautiful, healthy, positive things, and it will react accordingly.

Day 351   December 17

YOU KNOW WHAT to do: "stand and believe." There is a fine line here because we do need to do what we know to do to correct a problem, but there is a time when we stop what we are doing and wait for God. My rule of thumb is if I find myself fretting and striving, I have probably done all I know to do, and it is time to stop and just believe. But by the same token, I have watched Christians "waiting on God" when there are lots of things they could be doing. Find this important balance by asking God to keep you in line.

"GOD HAS A plan for your life, a plan to prosper you and not to harm you." Every single one of us was designed for a unique purpose in life, and when we do not fulfill that significant purpose, we will never be fulfilled. Without a meaningful purpose, life is boring and loses significance. Stir yourself up and be a big force in your own life. Remember your passion will usually point to your purpose, and if you're passionate about something, try to find a way to incorporate it into your profession.

DAY 352   December 18

WE LIVE IN a bizarre world. "Good is called evil, and evil is called good." I never thought I would live to see the day this prophetic Word would be fulfilled. As Christians, we are called to reconcile with a broken, tweaked, upside down world, where anything goes if it does not include the word Jesus! Witchcraft, birth control, alternate life-styles, all can be taught in public schools, while prayer and crosses are banned! We need to pray folks. "If my people who are called by my name will humble themselves and seek my face, I will heal their land." Pray and seek his face. We need a healing in this land like never before.

"FRET NOT, IT will only cause harm." Fretting is not only nonproductive and a waste of precious time, but it also causes harm! The phrase "fear not" are in the Bible 365 times—one time for every day of the year. Do you think maybe God was trying to get a point across? Studies have proven fretting is directly related to almost every illness known to man. Do not allow your mind to participate in this destructive habit. A better choice is to give it to God. "His yoke is easy, and his burden is light."

DAY 353   December 19

THE SCRIPTURES SAY, "Man is fearfully and wonderfully made." There is a purpose for everything. "Nature itself displays God." If you watch an expectant mother in the animal world, their instincts are amazing. They not only know how to care for their young, but they know how to care for their own bodily needs. They even know how to birth their own baby and what to do after the birth without any help from man. Listen to your body! The medical profession is wonderful for trauma, but God is ultimately the great healer. Look to him rather than man. He never lets those down who trust him, and he never makes mistakes, either!

NEGATIVE WORDS LEAD to negative actions, while positive words lead to positive actions. There is a book called *Change Your Words, Change Your Life*. And I totally believe this is true. "The power of life and death is in your tongue." Just imagine: this small member of your body can set your life on a course of destruction, or it can serve to elevate, encourage, and comfort. "Pleasant words are like a honeycomb, sweet to the soul and healing to all the flesh."

DAY 354   December 20

TERRIBLE THINGS CAN happen to you even when you serve God. We live in a fallen world, and we are all subject to the same pitfalls. But the good news is, when you serve God, he will see you through everything and strengthen you and make a better, stronger person out of you for having gone through the trial. Those who don't know how to put their trust in God will usually come out of a terrible situation bitter, angry, and weak. "Those who put their trust in God will never be disappointed."

NAME YOUR PAST and call it what it is. Own it, feel it, embrace the pain, and do not deny your situation. It is what it is! And it does not define you. The Word says we "overcome the enemy by the blood of the lamb and the word of our testimony." Your muddied past is an amazing tool that can be used to help yourself and others overcome the trials of the troubled world where we live. Do not allow pride or shame to rob you of the blessing that telling your story can bring, and remember to celebrate the mini, partial victories as you walk through your trial. Share your testimony!

Day 355   December 21

DO NOT ALLOW yourself to get caught up in the worldly trappings of Christmas. The world's celebration of Christmas is fun, festive, and exciting, but be sure to remember the real reason for the season. It is fun to participate in the exciting festivities, and it is good to do so because this is the one time of the year the world is on the same page with Christians. But their worldly celebration should never trump our truth. Let the true wonder of Christmas shine through you. "Jesus is the reason for the season."

YOU NEED TO execute today what you want to celebrate tomorrow. Because your celebrations tomorrow depend on what you do today. It is up to you to make your celebrations for tomorrow. "Acknowledge God in all your ways, and he will direct your path." But God can only direct the path of those who are moving.

Day 356   December 22

HURRY CAN DESTROY our joy. Don't just skim the surface of life as you scurry around, but rather unclutter and savor your life! There is always something to do, and worthy projects abound, but we can't do everything, and it is foolish to try. We will never do our best when we are rushing around trying to fit everything in. This Christmas season, slow down and pay attention to the things that really matter. Prioritize your life and remember "Jesus is the reason for the season."

"IF YOU SEEK God's will in everything you do, he will show you which path to take." There is such a comfort in knowing God is your navigator and your GPS, and he never makes mistakes. But the key is to trust him in everything, and when you have done that, rest assured you will automatically know which path to take. A path that will be void of any evil thing, a path strewn with treasures at every turn, a path filled with peace and joy, and a path that ultimately leads to paradise.

Day 357   December 23

THE WORLD IS full of offenses, and if you choose to receive offenses, it will stunt your growth. There is absolutely nothing beneficial in taking offense to what others have said that may or may not have been meant to insult you. If a word comes out against you that is not true, God's Word says it will go back on the one who sent it. Be willing to give others the benefit of the doubt. It's God's battle, not yours.

SOMETIMES THINGS START out great, but there are bound to be setbacks and discouragements. Whenever things are going really good, the enemy will often stir up trouble. When this happens, take charge against it. Call on God, go to prayer, and guard against demonic influences that will often include division. If you live within the parameters of God's Word, you can be assured God will stand for you. Go towards the threat with a plan to defend your faith and your family. Set a plan in place in case you are struck by temptation. Always be ready to defend. "No weapon formed against you will prosper, and every word that comes out against you will go back on the one who sent it."

Day 358   December 24

OUR SPIRITUAL MALADY is separation. And our remedy is connection. We all seek connection, but who we connect to will determine the direction of our lives and our lives' outcomes. Connection to God, through the heart of Jesus, is the rock I choose to build my life upon. The beautiful and ofttimes hidden meaning of Christmas is the perfect time to make this life-changing connection. My prayer for you and yours for this Christmas season is that you will be surrounded with the beauty and splendor of the true meaning of Christmas.

"TRUST GOD WITH all your heart and lean not on your own understanding, and he will direct your path." I am convinced we rarely trust God with ALL our heart, and we almost always try to figure things out ourselves. This is the main cause of why things go amok in our lives. Make a conscious effort to totally trust God and to defy the tendency to do things your own way. "Those who put their trust in God will never be disappointed."

DAY 359   December 25

WHAT DOES CHRISTMAS mean to you? Is it just a wonderful holiday when everybody gets presents, decorates their house with lights, and goes to Christmas parties? We all love the festivities of Christmas, but the meaning of this day holds a true treasure in the heart of those who understand what this day really stands for. It is doubtful December 25 is the actual birthdate of Christ, but it is the day we celebrate his birthday. Take the time this Christmas season to meditate on the magnitude of what this day has meant to mankind. Have a blessed Christmas.

GREAT PEOPLE ARE ordinary people who make great decisions. Knowing God and honoring him is the most important decision in your life. Decide in advance how you will react to any given situation, and then stick to what you know to be right. A simple "help me, Lord" can determine the difference between a decision that will catapult you right to the top or send you crashing right to the bottom. "Acknowledge God in all your ways and he will make your path straight."

DAY 360   December 26

INIQUITY IS THE knowing violation of established law. Iniquity is different than sin. Iniquity is knowing it is sin and still choosing to do it. America, and even the Church, is participating in iniquity. They are compromising even when they know the truth. Endure till the end. Take a stand against the things that are wrong. Do not enter in, even though it is so easy to flow along with the crowd. That crowd is flowing right into hell. The gates are wide, and many shall go thereof. Make a decision to endure and take the narrow path. Always stand for truth and integrity, even if it means your team loses.

JUST BECAUSE YOUR faith waivers and fails for a season does not mean you are not saved. This happens at one time or another to most believers. Be encouraged and draw near to God, and he will draw near to you. Just because you do not feel God is near you does not mean he is not there. "I will never leave you or forsake you."

Day 361   December 27

STUDIES HAVE BEEN done that prove when we lie down at night to go to sleep, if we will acknowledge at least two things we are grateful for in that day, we will not only go to sleep faster, but we will stay asleep! Are you aware that more people have insomnia than not? This should be a blessing to everyone. What a simple way to alleviate insomnia. "Be grateful for everything. This is God's will for you." Sweet sleep!

SADNESS OF HEART can be seen on the face. Be attentive to those who look worried or weary. Life has many troubles, and your consideration of others during these times can be so much help. Tending to the concerns of others is healthy for you because it keeps your mind off your own problems and will make you feel grateful and lift your self-worth. God tells us to "consider others more important than yourself." If everyone really did that, the world would be a much better place. Let's do our part.

DAY 362   December 28

DON'T YOU JUST love a good backfire? When someone is trying to destroy someone else, and it backfires on them and works towards good for their intended target. This is God's Word at work. He says, "Whatever you sow, you shall reap." Those who lie, steal, gossip, or cheat are throwing out a boomerang that will come back on them like a Mack truck. The same is true in the reverse. When you do something good for others, God promises he will do something good for you. Play nice!

"SOME TRUST IN horses, some trust in chariots, but we trust in the Lord." Faith in God will always overcome in the end. Sometimes it isn't even necessary to fight back. If you are doing what is right and you are honoring God as you do it, God says, "Those who wage war against you will perish." When evil surrounds you, keep looking to God and believing his Word. Praise him in the midst of the trouble! We trust the Lord, how can we lose?

DAY 363   December 29

ALL OF US are guilty of taking things for granted. When we get a new car, we are thrilled and excited, and we really appreciate it. But how long does it take before that new car becomes old stuff, and we don't even notice it anymore? This is what we do with everything in our life. We just take it for granted. Remember appreciation is probably the greatest gift on the planet. You can have all the worldly goods in the world, but if you do not have the gift of appreciation, you have nothing! "Give thanks in every circumstance." Gratitude and gratefulness are truly rare and coveted gems.

EVERYTHING DONE FOR God should be respected, even if it does not agree with your belief. Remember that the Word says, "Seek and you shall find." So whenever you see someone seeking the spiritual realm in any form, trust they will find the truth. Many of us try several paths before the right one appears. Be patient with loved ones who seem to be going in the wrong direction. Pray for them and trust that if they are seeking, God will move them towards the truth. Don't beat them over the head with your Bible, either; set a good example with your own behavior and respect their stance.

DAY 364   December 30

YOU ARE WHO the Bible says you are. You are God's treasure, and "he knew your name even before you were born." Even if you choose not to acknowledge God, he still loves you. There are many who will never know the love of their Father in heaven, and he will never push himself on you, but "if you draw close to him, he will draw close to you." Getting to know God in this life is the greatest decision I have ever made. The treasures he shows his children as we walk out this complicated journey we call life is the biggest jackpot you will ever hit!

"SILENCE IN THE face of evil is evil itself." When you see evil being done and you choose not to get involved, you are guilty by association. God tells us to "defend those who cannot defend themselves." Apathy is a grievous character trait. Choose to be someone who stands up for what is right and concerns themselves more with what God thinks than with what man thinks. "If God be for you, who can be against you?"

Day 365   December 31

SAY THE NAME of Jesus, and he will come to where you are. You don't have to go to where he is. He knows right where you are. If you find yourself in a place that you don't know what to do or a place where you are frightened or unhappy, just say the name Jesus. You don't have to say any more than that. When you call his name, he will be there with you. I don't know about you, but that utterly comforts me. Jesus, Jesus, Jesus.

PSALM 118:6 SAYS, "The Lord is for me, so I will have no fear. What can mere people do to me?" I love that scripture! When you trust God as your Lord, you are in the palm of his hand, and no one can do anything to you without his permission. Never fear man, but rather fear your Father in heaven. The fear you feel for God should be a healthy fear rooted in love and respect. With this respect comes a blessed certainty that all is well. "Call unto God, and he will deliver you from all your fears."

Parting Thoughts

MY EARLY YEARS were filled with fear and anxiety, and throughout my life I was known for loving and memorizing poems. In my early twenties, I found a poem I decided to base my life on. It was written by Ralph Waldo Emerson. The first time I read it, I was so taken by its determination to see the beauty in everything. I memorized it, and I couldn't even begin to count how many times I have recited it over the years to anyone who would listen. It has become my mantra, my choice, and I have walked this out as I choose to see the beauty, even in the "mud and scum of things."

Music

Let me go where'er I will,
I hear a sky-born music still:
It sounds from all things old,
It sounds from all things young,
From all that's fair, from all that's foul,
Peals out a cheerful song.

It is not only in the rose,
It is not only in the bird,
Not only where the rainbow glows,
Nor in the song of woman heard,

But in the darkest, meanest things
There alway, alway something sings.

'T is not in the high stars alone,
Nor in the cup of budding flowers,
Nor in the redbreast's mellow tone,
Nor in the bow that smiles in showers,
But in the mud and scum of things
There alway, alway something sings.

Philippians 4:8 says, "Whatever is true, whatever is honorable, whatever is just, whatever is pure, whatever is lovely or commendable, if there is any excellence, if there is anything worthy of praise, think about these things."

Velma

The Bridge Builder

BY WILL ALLEN DROMGOOLE

An old man going a lone highway,
Came, at the evening cold and gray,
To a chasm vast and deep and wide.
Through which was flowing a sullen tide
The old man crossed in the twilight dim,
The sullen stream had no fear for him;
But he turned when safe on the other side
And built a bridge to span the tide.

"Old man," said a fellow pilgrim near,
"You are wasting your strength with building here;
Your journey will end with the ending day,
You never again will pass this way;
You've crossed the chasm, deep and wide,
Why build this bridge at evening tide?"

The builder lifted his old gray head;
"Good friend, in the path I have come," he said,
"There followed after me to-day
A youth whose feet must pass this way.
This chasm that has been as naught to me
To that fair-haired youth may a pitfall be;
He, too, must cross in the twilight dim;
Good friend, I am building this bridge for him!"

CPSIA information can be obtained
at www.ICGtesting.com
Printed in the USA
LVHW040020280921
698843LV00002B/15